D0209413

# the series on school reform



Teaching Youth Media: A Critical Guide to Literacy, Video Production, & Social Change
STEVEN GOODMAN

Inside the National Writing Project: Connecting Network Learning and Classrooms
ANN LIEBERMAN AND DIANE WOOD

Standards Reform in High-Poverty Schools: Managing Conflict and Building Capacity
CAROL A. BARNES

Standards of Mind and Heart: Creating the Good High School
PEGGY SILVA AND ROBERT A. MACKIN

Upstart Startup: Creating and Sustaining a Public Charter School
JAMES NEHRING

One Kid at a Time: Big Lessons from a Small School
ELIOT LEVINE

Guiding School Change: The Role and Work of Change Agents
FRANCES O'CONNELL RUST AND HELEN FREIDUS, EDITORS

Teachers Caught in the Action: Professional Development That Matters
ANN LIEBERMAN AND LYNNE MILLER, EDITORS

The Competent Classroom: Aligning High School Curriculum, Standards, and Assessment—A Creative Teaching Guide
ALLISON ZMUDA AND MARY TOMAINO

Central Park East and Its Graduates: "Learning by Heart"
DAVID BENSMAN

Taking Charge of Curriculum: Teacher Networks and Curriculum Implementation
JACOB E. ADAMS, JR.

Teaching With Power: Shared Decision-Making and Classroom Practice
CAROL REED

Good Schools/Real Schools: Why School Reform Doesn't Last
DEAN FINK

Beyond Formulas in Mathematics and Teaching: Dynamics of the High School Algebra Classroom
DANIEL CHAZAN

School Reform Behind the Scenes
JOSEPH P. McDONALD, THOMAS HATCH, EDWARD KIRBY, NANCY AMES, NORRIS M. HAYNES, AND EDWARD T. JOYNER

Looking Together at Student Work: A Companion Guide to *Assessing Student Learning*
TINA BLYTHE, DAVID ALLEN, AND BARBARA SHIEFFELIN POWELL

Looking at Student Work: A Window into the Classroom (Video)
ANNENBERG INSTITUTE FOR SCHOOL REFORM

Teachers—Transforming Their World and Their Work
ANN LIEBERMAN AND LYNNE MILLER

Teaching in Common: Challenges to Joint Work in Classrooms and Schools
ANNE DiPARDO

Charter Schools: Another Flawed Educational Reform?
SEYMOUR B. SARASON

Assessing Student Learning: From Grading to Understanding
DAVID ALLEN, EDITOR

Racing with the Clock: Making Time for Teaching and Learning in School Reform
NANCY E. ADELMAN, KAREN PANTON WALKING EAGLE, AND ANDY HARGREAVES, EDITORS

The Role of State Departments of Education in Complex School Reform
SUSAN FOLLETT LUSI

Making Professional Development Schools Work: Politics, Practice, and Policy
MARSHA LEVINE AND ROBERTA TRACHTMAN, EDITORS

*(Continued)*

**the series on school reform,** *continued*

How It Works—Inside a School–College Collaboration
SIDNEY TRUBOWITZ AND PAUL LONGO

Surviving School Reform: A Year in the Life of One School
LARAINE K. HONG

Eyes on the Child: Three Portfolio Stories
KATHE JERVIS

Revisiting "The Culture of the School and the Problem of Change"
SEYMOUR B. SARASON

Teacher Learning: New Policies, New Practices
MILBREY W. McLAUGHLIN AND IDA OBERMAN, EDITORS

What's Happening in Math Class? Envisioning New Practices Through Teacher Narratives (Volume 1)
DEBORAH SCHIFTER, EDITOR

What's Happening in Math Class? Reconstructing Professional Identities (Volume 2)
DEBORAH SCHIFTER, EDITOR

The Subjects in Question: Departmental Organization and the High School
LESLIE SANTEE SISKIN AND JUDITH WARREN LITTLE, EDITORS

Authentic Assessment in Action: Studies of Schools and Students at Work
LINDA DARLING-HAMMOND, JACQUELINE ANCESS, AND BEVERLY FALK

School Work: Gender and the Cultural Construction of Teaching
SARI KNOPP BIKLEN

School Change: The Personal Development of a Point of View
SEYMOUR B. SARASON

The Work of Restructuring Schools: Building from the Ground Up
ANN LIEBERMAN, EDITOR

Stirring the Chalkdust: Tales of Teachers Changing Classroom Practice
PATRICIA A. WASLEY

# Teaching Youth Media

*A Critical Guide to Literacy, Video Production, & Social Change*

**STEVEN GOODMAN**

**Foreword by Maxine Greene**

Teachers College
Columbia University
New York and London

Published by Teachers College Press, 1234 Amsterdam Avenue, New York, NY 10027



*Chapter opening photographs by*: Chapter 1, Joseph Rodriguez; Chapters 2 and 3, Steven Goodman; Chapter 4, Torrance York. All photographs used with permission.

*Library of Congress Cataloging-in-Publication Data*

Goodman, Steven.
Teaching youth media : a critical guide to literacy, video production & social change/ Steven Goodman ; foreword by Maxine Greene.
p. cm. — (The series on school reform)
Includes bibliographical references and index.
ISBN 0-8077-4289-9 (cloth : alk. paper) — ISBN 0-8077-4288-0 (pbk. : alk. paper)
1. Mass media in education—United States. 2. Media literacy—United States. 3. Critical thinking. I. Title. II. Series.
LB1043 .G59 2002
371.33—dc21 2002073237

ISBN 0-8077-4288-0 (paper)
ISBN 0-8077-4289-9 (cloth)

Printed on acid-free paper

Manufactured in the United States of America

10 09 08 07 06 05 04 03 8 7 6 5 4 3 2 1

*This book is dedicated to my children,*
*Theodore and Amelia*

# *Contents*

# *Foreword*

MOST ADULTS ARE AWARE of the degree to which today's young people (especially those who are poverty-ridden) are enmeshed in a visual and oral media culture rather than the print-based culture long associated with literacy. Few, though, have confronted the degree to which this change has created a language gap—what Goodman calls a disconnect between the experiences of the young and the print culture prevailing in high schools. This ground-breaking book not only explains the consequences thereof, but also presents a view of critical literacy that may well close this gap. Such necessary steps do not imply that the teaching of print literacy should be set aside. Goodman is well aware that a mastery of the written word is necessary for coping with and making sense of an increasingly complex world. But a long engagement with urban high schools and young people has convinced him of the felt irrelevance of existing curricula.

He is proposing (and demonstrating) a new and suggestive way of rendering schools more learner-centered and community-based. The idea is that if youngsters are provided opportunities to look at and reflect upon the environments surrounding them and the social relations in which they are involved, they might become critically literate in a way that might enable them to close the language gap. One of the exciting things about this text is how Goodman describes the development of visual and oral literacy from the vantage point of an experienced teacher and maker of documentary videos. He offers his readers a pedagogy he himself uses to engage students in learning the craft of making their own videos; and there is something very meaningful in a pedagogy that links "making" to "a visual grasping," an opening to new understanding. It is in the spirit of a Deweyan "learning by doing"; and readers cannot but share with Steven Goodman the hope that such projects may become part of curricula in high schools seeking contact with those willing to learn more. As Goodman describes the Center where much of this takes place, he shows us the stress on techniques and skills and how skill learning can become important if exercised for the sake of a valuable end.

Techniques are not enough, however. Students are also asked to make choices among topics and themes important in their lives. Often this results in a showing forth of many kinds of suffering, of neglect, injustices, deficiencies. Oftentimes, students, lacking a way of saying or showing how things are with them (caught in what Paulo Freire would describe as a "deadly silence"), find themselves able to "name" and imagine how they might change their worlds for the first time as they capture it through a scene or narrative, a gesture or dialogue. Looking, as Goodman does, through a "critical lens," the reader cannot but "see" and take into account many kinds of violence on the streets, drug-dealing, the damage done by AIDS and abuse, the ubiquity of guns, the omnipresence of death. Going into concrete detail about the shaping and showing of a number of videos, Goodman is able to help readers become conscious of what it is like in housing projects and poverty-stricken neighborhoods—and what it takes to survive.

Because these realities are seen and projected from the viewpoints of young people who live and make their lives in such places, readers are taken beyond what even skilled ethnographers can reveal, becoming privy to interchanges, body movements, dialogues about things such as jail and drugs and "gunz." Goodman helps us to see why and how the nagging, personal questions arise—questions that cannot but lead in time to the use of the full range of literacies, including printed words, in all the diverse realms of meaning.

This book is remarkable and authentic in the light it casts on possible practice in a context of unfriendly neighborhoods and insufficient public schools. Goodman begins with an enlightening version of the history of literacy, from the day symbolic orders were created before the invention of the Gutenberg printing press. Doing so, he offers us a rich and fluid rendering of the shifting of meanings of literacy, even as he contributes to the reader's effort to reconcile the tradition of the printed word with the visual and oral, perhaps to allow all of us to expand and deepen our visions of the "real." This is a brilliant and exciting book. It may transform some corners of the world.

Maxine Greene
Teachers College
Columbia University

# Acknowledgments

THE ORIGINS OF THIS BOOK date back to conversations I had with Joe McDonald in 1995, while planning a national conference at Wingspread on media literacy, equity, and education reform. I was honored when he asked me to write a book capturing the ideas generated by that gathering. I am grateful to Margie Nicholson, Patricia Boero, Woody Wickham, and the John D. and Catherine T. MacArthur Foundation for supporting both the conference and the early development of this book. The project, though, grew considerably broader in scope, as I used the opportunity to try and make sense of my work at the intersection of media education, school reform, and social change. I am indebted to Joe for all the kind words of encouragement and guidance he so generously provided.

I am particularly grateful to Carole Saltz for inviting me to write my story for Teachers College Press about teaching youth media, and for coaching me along the way in writing it. Many thanks go to Catherine Bernard who despite all the editorial challenges that came up patiently worked to create some order out of the chaos of ideas I had spread across the manuscript. I would also like to thank Aureliano Vázquez, Jr., for all his assistance editing this book. I deeply admire and appreciate Maxine Greene, whose writing, speaking, and ceaseless agitating for a more just and humane system of schooling has been an inspiration for me to try in some small way to put her philosophy into practice at the Educational Video Center (EVC).

This book would never have come into being without the selfless assistance of my friend Bill Tally, who made invaluable contributions to the final structure and content of the book. Over the course of many spirited discussions, usually over pints of ale, Bill pushed me to deepen my thinking and make a larger argument about media literacy, education reform, and youth culture.

I greatly appreciate Norman Cowie and Kathleen Tyner for their insightful comments upon reviewing the manuscript, and JoEllen Fisherkeller for the moral and intellectual support she gave me throughout the process. I am forever indebted to Carolyn Cocca for the thorough reading and many improvements that she made to the final draft. I am very fortunate to have benefited from her powerful command of language and respect for the agency of the young people I write about.

The arguments and observations I make in this book grow out of the principles and practices of teaching youth media at EVC, many of them emerging from my experiences teaching video and producing documentaries in the early 1980s. I was lucky to be mentored by generous and gifted teachers at the alternative high school Satellite Academy—Forsyth Street, including Liz Andersen, Howard Friedman, Anthony Conelli, and the late Stephen Shapiro; and by the social documentary makers at Downtown Community TV Center, among them Jon Alpert, Keiko Tsuno, Karen Ranucci, Maryann Deleo, Hye Jung Park, Victor Sanchez, and Peter Kwong.

EVC grew from the germ of an idea into a reality only because of the many friends and family members who gave so much of their time and moral and material support in the early years, including Suzanne Valenza, Jeff Strange, Cathy Rieser, Kate Chieco, Marie Cirillo, Fran Barrett, Mark Weiss, Angie Karran, my brothers Ben and Alex, my sister Jackie, my mother Marion, and my late father Irving Goodman.

I truly appreciate the many committed educators and media activists whose ideas and work have informed and enriched EVC's theory and practice. A partial list follows: Marilyn Wentworth, Elliot Wigginton, Pat Wasley, Rick Lear, Keith Hefner, Marcie Wolfe, Hubert Dyosi, Bret Eynon, Lucy Calkins, Norm Fruchter, Barbara Cervone, Kathleen Cushman, Peter Kleinbard, Candy Systra, Stuart Ewen, George Stoney, Lillian Jimenez, Cara Mertes, Marty Lucas, Karen Helmerson, Robert Gipe, Dee Davis, Chris Bratton, Meghan McDermott, Terry Baker, Cornelia Brunner, Margaret Honey, and the late Jan Hawkins. My own thinking has also been influenced by the pioneering media education work of colleagues in England and Canada, such as Barry Duncan, David Buckingham, Julian Sefton-Green, Cary Bazelgette, and Jenny Grahame.

I would be remiss if I didn't acknowledge all the EVC staff and board members—past and present—who have contributed their time, creative energy, and ideas to building and sustaining the organization. I have learned so much from a staff whose intelligence, commitment, and humor in the face of difficult challenges has semester after semester, year after year, made it possible for kids to pick up a camera, ask thoughtful questions, and ultimately see the world through new eyes. I am deeply grateful to the board members, who have always been there for me and for EVC giving so much to ensure the vitality of the organization, in spite of the cuts in education and arts funding that have too often threatened to close our doors. There is not enough space to name all the staff and board members over the past eighteen years, but I would like to acknowledge those most current, including Caron Atlas, Christina Pantazis-Blades, Bruni

Burres, George Cocheran, Lisa Conrad, Julie Criniere, Jeremy Engle, Ivana Espinet, Barbara Fitts, Gail Gant, Cesar Guerra, Emily Hartzell, Kellon Innocent, Joan Jubela, Ron Litke, Amy Melnick, Christine Mendoza, Betsy Newman, Yvette Nieves, Carlos Pareja, Rebecca Renard, and Torrance York.

I am especially indebted to Dave Murdock who as a staff member, board member, and friend has been a trusted voice of intelligence and decency for over twenty years. His steadfast commitment to the intellectual, artistic, and social development of his students has immeasurably enriched the lives of all those he taught.

I would like to thank the many funders who have so generously supported EVC's work over the years, including the Aaron Diamond Foundation, Catalog for Giving, Charles Hayden Foundation, Funding Exchange-Lattimore J. Fund, H. M. and T. Cohn Foundation, JPMorgan Chase, Janet Stone Jones Foundation, Manhattan Neighborhood Network, The McGraw-Hill Companies, Nathan Cummings Foundation, National Endowment for the Arts, the New York City Department of Education's Superintendency for Alternative, Adult, and Continuing Education Schools and Programs, The New York City Community Trust, New York Foundation, New York State Council on the Arts, Open Society Institute, President's Committee on the Arts and the Humanities, Robert Bowne Foundation, Surdna Foundation, U.S. Department of Education, W. K. Kellogg Foundation, Wallace-Reader's Digest Funds, Wellspring Foundation, William Randolph Hearst Foundation, and individual donors.

I owe a huge debt of thanks to Alan Dichter and Nancy Mohr who from the earliest years of EVC have opened their home and hearts to nurture and tirelessly promote the center's work—and have always done so with humor and grace, asking for nothing in return. Their vast experience in school reform, authentic assessment, and professional development has helped EVC forge an enduring partnership with the New York City Alternative High Schools and has given EVC's work a rigor that would not have been possible otherwise.

There would be no book without the cooperation of the many students and teachers who graciously allowed me to videotape, interview, observe, and learn from them. Although their identity is necessarily hidden by pseudonyms, I would like to acknowledge some of them here: Raymond Ballinger, Schantyce Garrett, Joan Harmon, Joan Jubela, Amy Melnick, JoAnne Dilauro, and Bill Stroud.

Finally, I am thankful every day for my son Theodore and daughter Amelia who have taught me so much about children, literacy, and the media, and continue to be for me a delightful source of learning and joy.

# *Introduction*

I REMEMBER TAKING MY SON THEO to school on his orientation day for kindergarten. I sat awkwardly in his small wooden chair observing, along with the other parents, as the teacher began to lead an activity. She gathered all the children on the carpet and showed them a large picture book. "I know you can all read," she began with a big smile. "Who can tell me what this is?" she asked, pointing to a brightly colored shape on the page. Six or seven eager hands shot up. "It's a circle," one girl answered. "And this?" the teacher continued, pointing to the next shape. "It's a square, and that's a triangle." "Good, good," she said, turning the big page. "You all know about a lot of things already. Now who knows what this is?" Everyone recognized the yellow curves. "It's McDonald's!" they shouted in a chorus. "And that's Burger King! And Toys 'Я' Us!"

My jaw dropped. I could understand that she wanted to build the children's confidence as beginning readers, but I couldn't believe that she was using their recognition of commercial logos to do this, as if they didn't already get enough exposure to these signs and symbols everywhere else outside of school. Learning to read books was quite a different matter from learning to buy things.

But the more I thought about it, the more it made sense. These five-year-olds could not yet read or write printed words (aside from their own names), but they could already read these signs. Today's explosion in media technologies has brought new literacies into being, transforming the way these kindergarteners read the word and read the world, even if our schools have been one of the last places to recognize this. These children have been learning the language of our mass media culture since infancy, growing up on a steady diet of visual, aural, and print media messages. The media is now competing with the family and school to become their master storyteller and teacher.

The media saturation of most kids' everyday lives has been well documented. Children ages eight and older spend the equivalent of a full work week—an average of 6¾ hours per day—in front of a screen of some kind of electronic media. Increasingly, they need go no further than their bedrooms to consume their media of choice. Two-thirds of children eight and older and one-third of preschoolers have a television in their bedrooms (The Henry J. Kaiser Family Foundation, 1999). In just an hour of television, a child can watch as many as many as 1,200 different images (Postman, 1994), and across the natural course of each day's experiences, he is exposed to countless thousands more mass media messages. While the precise impact of this media consumption is subject to debate, it is clear that over time, as these messages are repeated in numerous forms day in and day out, they contribute to young people's evolving sense of identity, community, and worldview.

I work with inner-city teenagers who have been raised for some fifteen years on the messages, stories, and lessons of the commercial media. As founding director of the Educational Video Center (EVC), a community-based media center in New York City, I have been privileged to teach and learn from the hundreds of young people who have made documentaries in our workshops over the years. These students have given me a window into the multiple worlds in which they live: the mainstream world of global media entertainment and consumption; the marginalized world of the poor, mostly African American and Latino community; and the all-too-fossilized world of the large urban schools, most of which fail to acknowledge or teach them about either of the other two realms.

One thing that has struck me in my work with urban kids is the odd congruence between two very different systems: the system of global media that wants young people to be spectators and consumers rather than social actors, and a factory system of schooling that wants young people to be passive and willing vessels for a prescribed set of knowledge and skills. For poor and minority children, a third system is congruent with the first two: a social and political order that wants to monitor and control their behavior in order to minimize risks to the white, middle-class community. Although the content of these systems differs greatly, their form, structure, and outcomes are oddly parallel. They all are one-way systems that seek to repress the agency and self-determination of young people.

The failure of schools and after-school programs to address the media as the predominant language of youth today, or to recognize the social and cultural contexts in which students live, has resulted in a profound disconnect. It's a disconnect that occurs between the experiences that most students have during their time in school and those they have during their time outside of school. Until corrected, this disconnect will lead to the increased alienation of low-income urban youth from the dominant social, political, and economic mainstream. Their voices will be muted, their chances to move up and out of poverty will be greatly diminished, and society at large will be that much poorer for the lack of all the creative potential that went unrealized.

Educators, youth development workers, and everyone else who cares about the well-being of these kids need to develop a deeper and nuanced understanding of the forces that shape their lives—our media and consumer culture and our systems of schooling and juvenile justice—as well as a genuine respect for the creative problem-solving capacities of low-income students and their communities. So, in addition to the myriad individual "life skills" that are typically offered to at-risk kids, they need to be engaged in the study of the systemic roadblocks in their way—such as police brutality, unequal educational resources, substandard housing, and so on—and what sort of collective action they might take to move those roadblocks aside.

More specifically, I am arguing for schools and after-school programs to help these youths develop the skills and habits required for what I call a "critical literacy." By that I mean the ability to analyze, evaluate, and produce print, aural, and visual forms of communication. A critical literacy empowers low-income, urban teenagers to understand how media is made to convey particular messages and how they can use electronic and print technologies themselves to document and publicly voice their ideas and concerns regarding the most important issues in their lives.

Taking a video camera into the community as a regular method for teaching and learning gives kids a critical lens through which they can explore the world around them. It helps them to defamiliarize the familiar taken-for-granted conditions of life. This approach to critical literacy links media analysis to production; learning about the world is directly linked to the possibility of changing it. Command of literacy in this sense is not only a matter of performing well on standardized tests; it is a prerequisite for self-representation and autonomous citizenship.

Over the past 20 years that I have worked with New York City teenagers, a number of questions (to which there are probably no answers) have continually resurfaced for me and my colleagues at EVC, prompting us each time to look more closely at the problems and possibilities of this model of media education. Among those questions are: How do students' out-of-school experiences learning from the media and their local community shape the kinds of literacies and critical thinking skills they bring with them to school each day? What challenges do teachers and youth workers face in engaging students in community inquiry projects that include both media analysis and production? What has been the history of prior efforts to teach with and about media and technology? How can we broaden the impact of this model by bringing it to scale in a variety of school and after-school community settings? And finally, in studying the array of cultural, economic, and social contradictions that shape the world of urban teenagers, how can we use that new understanding to support these young people as they struggle through those contradictions to reach their full intellectual and creative potential?

My journey to find answers to these questions has been immeasurably aided and informed by a number of sources, including colleagues in teaching, youth development, media, and university research; historical literature on the role of literacy and mass media in Western societies; and sociological work on urban youth and school reform. But I have learned the most from my experience observing and talking with the students in EVC programs, their teachers, and of course my two children, who teach me every day about the world of media in which they are growing up. This book describes some of what I have learned along the way.

## CRITICAL LITERACY: READING THE DOMINANT MEDIUM

Historically, the way in which poor and other marginalized groups have managed to become visible, to demand political recognition and economic rights, has been through the acquisition of literacy in the dominant medium. However, the dominant medium is changing. Learning to read and write the printed word is still essential, but is no longer sufficient in a world where television, radio, movies, videos, magazines, and the World Wide Web have all become powerful and pervasive sites for public education and literacy. Students need to develop a critical literacy to read this broad array of media.

Out of these competing and overlapping modes of mass communication, the dominant form of language has become the image. The image—still and moving, black-and-white and color, chemically developed and electronically scanned, broadcast and downloaded, analog and digital—has been transforming and overshadowing the printed word. In fact, with the explosion of the Internet and web-based communication, computer-generated graphic design and printing has in many respects turned the printed word *into* image. Our experience of human relations, nature, material things, and ideas has become increasingly flattened into this two-dimensional world. As cultural critic Sven Bikerts (1994) describes it, "a communications net, a soft and pliable mesh woven from invisible threads, has fallen over everything. The so-called natural world, the place we used to live, which served us so long as the yardstick for all measurements, can now only be perceived through a scrim" (p. 120).

The profound changes in our culture of literacy wrought by the progressive march of the image technologies across the 20th century invite comparison with the historic moment when the invention of the Gutenberg printing press upturned 15th-century Europe. However, mass communication in our contemporary culture might arguably bear greater similarity with the late 10th century, when there was a revival of the image, not the word. Following Pope Gregory the Great's famous dictum, "Painting can do for the illiterate what writing does for those who can read" (Shlain, 1998, p. 266), theologians used church paintings, sculptures, and the very church buildings themselves as a form of collective communication to teach the Bible to the unlettered masses. The medieval eye read everything in nature as a kind of symbolic alphabet through which God spoke and revealed the order of things (Eco, 1986).

Within the context of our 21st-century media culture, the language of images also tells stories and teaches lessons about the order of things. However, today's symbols are most commonly used to teach that the promise of salvation is brought about through material acquisition instead of spiritual devotion.

Pope Gregory would certainly have been in awe of the way the images and stories of advertising so completely fill the electronic screens and physical spaces of our daily life today. There is a continuity and uninterrupted flow that connects all our visual experiences—both private and public—so that that a stroll down an urban street is like a walk through a shopping mall, which is like even the briefest time spent watching television. The same images are repeated over and over.

Not unlike the medieval church, our temples of communications and commerce use a complex language of codes and conventions across various genres to tell contemporary stories of virtue and vice. While some genres are mainly intended to be persuasive (such as commercials), narrative (such as movies), or descriptive (such as news photos accompanying articles), they all tell stories of one kind or another. The storyteller makes countless decisions throughout the media production process, each of which plays a role in shaping the kind of meaning a particular audience makes out of what they listen to and watch. It is important to recognize, however, that audiences actively interpret and understand these media stories in different ways, often constructing different meanings than what the storyteller intended (Fisherkeller, 2002, p. 13). Even though they may appear to the viewer as natural or unintended, these elements are the result of conscious choices (artistic, financial, or logistical) on the part of the media makers, such as whether to shoot in film or video, black and white or color, in close-up or wide angle, from street level or a helicopter's perspective, handheld or on a tripod, in a studio or on location, with music and sound effects added or without, lit with bright colors or in shadow. These are all part of the grammar that makes up the language of media.

Children learn to read the symbolic alphabet of the mass media long before they learn to read words, understanding that golden arches, Nike swooshes, and the like carry messages that have to do with getting stuff such as Happy Meal Disney characters, sneakers, dolls, or toys. Huge amounts of money and effort are invested in making kids literate in the language of consumerism and so apprenticing them for a lifetime of consumption. More than $2 billion is spent annually on advertising directed at children, over 20 times the amount spent just 10 years ago (Resse, 1998). These throw-away commodities are the currency of childhood.

As kids grow up to become more voracious consumers of media and the stories and products it sells, educators need to recognize the importance of teaching their students to be more critical of the media they are consuming. Acknowledging this allows teachers to make the media a part of their curriculum for students to learn to read and produce. Close study reveals how all images are constructed and change as the pictures are cropped, disassembled, and reassembled. Adding different captions to a still photo changes its perceived meaning, as does adding different music or narration to video images. Whole stories can be told using only images, and are interpreted differently by different viewers.

Among the most effective strategies for teaching critical literacy is for students to create their own media. Then they can begin to understand through their own experience the multiple layers of data that make up the television or [illegible] azines they read. They can see for thems [illegible] or added to sentences and made to seem [illegible] spoken that way; how causes and effects [illegible]; and how perceptions of time, space, po [illegible] ed without seeming to be. With a critical [illegible] erstand how the media acts as a frame a [illegible] ppearing to be a clear window.

Teaching crit [illegible] udents grow into adolescence and can grasp more abstract concepts, but it is also more complicated, as they become consumers of news. They are growing up in a media culture of spectacle that has normalized the notion that entertainment is news and news is entertainment. It has become a given that the media is a business and that in order to produce high audience ratings and readership numbers, it must transform as much as it can into gripping, personal drama. One result is that a steady parade of dramas on a global scale (starring real-life heroes, villains, and victims such as O.J. Simpson, Saddam Hussein, Princess Diana, Monica Lewinsky, Bill Clinton, Rudy Giuliani, and Osama bin Laden) has come to dominate the national conversation for months at time.

Such a critical literacy gives students the analytic tools to read a commercial or a movie, and also to understand the big picture: how the media's overriding objective of getting and satisfying an audience tends to convert politics, warfare, religion, crime, and all aspects of our society into branches of show business (Gabler, 1998). And it must also be about creating spaces and modes of communication that are alternatives to the ratings-driven show business model of media making.

It struck me that my son Theo's teacher could actually be taking the children along a quite interesting exploration of visual language in our culture. But she took things no further than the simple recognition of signs and symbols. I would guess that learning to teach in this way was not part of any of the early childhood courses she took, nor was it likely to have been part of middle or high school pre-service teacher courses. But it certainly *could* be a part of standard classroom practice to teach kids to produce their own media and to analyze the symbols that they recognize and read every day—and will continue to recognize and read for the rest of their lives.

I was disappointed—but not surprised—by the missed learning opportunity in Theo's class. I wondered if over the next 13 years of his schooling, Theo's teachers would ever challenge him to peel back the linguistic and cultural layers of the signs and messages of our mass media. While this remains an open question, I knew for certain that his time *outside* of school would continue to be filled with the data of our media-saturated culture.

I also knew that the problem would be even greater for poor urban, mostly African American and Latino kids. Like middle-class students, they would most likely go to schools that teach literacy and academic skills in ways that ignore the educative role of the global commercial media. Unlike middle-class students, marginalized youth would also have to endure schools that fail to develop their print literacy skills and that dismiss the roles that their community's cultural traditions and social struggles play as agents of their intellectual and social development.

Failing to distribute critical literacy skills equally to all children—regardless of their race, class, gender, and ethnicity—only reinforces and perpetuates the inequities in knowledge and power that marginalized groups already face. This failure is endemic, particularly in the large urban schools across the country. Despite the best intentions of the teachers who work in them, these are institutions stuck in an old factory system of education. They have been stubbornly resistant to EVC's community-based approach to media education, as well as to other learner-centered reforms. Knowing something about how schools came to be the way they are might give us a fighting chance at changing them into institutions that use literacy to advance the struggle for greater equity and freedom in students' lives. It is therefore worth taking a brief look at the history of school structures and how that history impacts on what students learn, and what they do not learn, in the classroom today.

## THE FACTORY SYSTEM OF SCHOOLING

The generation of educators who built our nation's schools in the early 19th century was deeply influenced by the systemic order and efficiency achieved by the emerging industries of the era: the division of labor in the factory, the punctuality of the railroad, the chain of command and coordination in modern businesses. The confluence of immigration and urbanization had brought masses of children to American cities from impoverished farms on both sides of the Atlantic. The emerging social and industrial order counted on schools to instill discipline in them. "The important job of schools was to build good industrial habits. . . . Everything within the school had to be reduced to rigid routine" (Tyack, 1974, p. 46).

Efficiency and order became the controlling idea. The conveyor belt—the machine that transformed workers into assembly-line slaves of time and motion—became an organizing model: students (the raw material) were moved from class to class along the production line of school as specialized knowledge from each subject area (value) was added to them. Exams became the method for determining the quality of the product produced.

In the first decades of the 19th century, New York City philanthropists learned of a new school model for poor children that was designed by Joseph Lancaster in England. Lancaster argued that like the manager of a cotton mill, the superintendent of schools could supervise employees, keep the enterprise technically up to date, and monitor the uniformity and quality of the product. In the Lancaster model, a class of 450 pupils would be run by one master who would sit on a raised platform in the front of the large open room and receive the aid of monitors assigned to different sections. During the course of the school day, the students would be marched from one section to another, receiving instruction from each monitor. The monitors were in essence just points on the education assembly line (Spring, 1972).

Wealthy merchants and financiers argued that the factory atmosphere of this system was ideal training for a developing industrial society. Movement from section to section and instruction in large numbers required orderliness and precise habits on the part of the students. Handbooks were written that gave detailed instruction in such things as passing out books. When the Boston School Committee investigated the New York Lancaster schools in 1828, it reported that "its effects on the habits, character, and intelligence of youth are highly beneficial; disposing their minds to industry, to readiness of attention, and to subordination, thereby creating in early life a love of order, preparation for business" (Spring, 1972, pp. 45–46). This particular model was perpetuated into the 20th century by William Bagley, whose book *Classroom Management* became a standard teacher training text and was reprinted 30 times between 1907 and 1927.

But Lancaster's system did not go unchallenged. A different model, shaped by the work of John Dewey, sought to counter Lancaster's with a school that was built on cooperative group work. According to Dewey, the march of industrialization had destroyed the community system that existed on the family farm. In place of that community system, Dewey argued, there was only the alienated world of factory life and urban society. He believed that school must become as much of a social experience as it was an intellectual one, a community building force, one that could give meaning to the fragmented world of modern man. And so he emphasized cooperative group work throughout the school experience. In his view, school needed to be a place where students could gain practice in forming and testing moral and social judgments. It should be about cultivating independent-minded, critical-thinking citizens capable of solving social problems. It depended on the development of relationships among students, between students and teachers, and between students and the community. It was schooling for democracy (Dewey 1916, 1976).

Today's debates about the practices and purposes of our nation's schools are still influenced by the Lancaster/Dewey debate. Although the march of deindustrialization, globalization, and the information age has led to the closing and relocation of factories across the country, schools remain closely tied to the interests of business leaders. The success or failure of a school is still measured by how well it functions at producing literate workers for the new economy. High schools are still organized according to the conveyer-belt model of moving children along from subject to subject, pouring information into them as they pass by. They are still driven by the need for greater efficiency, as exemplified by the wave of standardized testing that has swept the nation. Despite the introduction of curricular innovations such as thematic, interdisciplinary learning, schools are still dominated by division of labor, specialization of knowledge, separation of school from community and of knowledge from experience.

## ATTEMPTS TO GO BEYOND THE FACTORY SYSTEM: TEACHING WITH AND ABOUT THE MEDIA

There is a critical factor that did not exist a century ago: the mass media culture. This force has grown to challenge and supersede the role of school as a powerful socializing influence on our nation's children, shaping their values, beliefs, and habits of mind. Given the prevalence of the media in their in-school and out-of-school lives, it is particularly worrisome that the factory system of education still has such a firm grip on American schools while media education has had such a marginal impact.

Nevertheless, there have been important media-related trends in education that have flowed through and around the factory system, causing some changes in approaches to education. In particular, three strands of media education—*technology integration, media literacy,* and *community media arts*—have made a mark on the broader landscape of school and community-based education.

The Educational Video Center's model of work has roots in each of these three aspects of media education. It is useful to have a sense of the history of the ideas and practices of each of these trends in order to consider how far they have brought us in teaching kids to critically understand and speak the language in which they are immersed, the language of the image. It's also important to think about how much further we have to go.

### Technology Integration

Technology integration has historically occupied the instrumental wing of the media education field. From this perspective, technology has been promoted as a highly efficient instrument that can aid teachers in delivering information to students. This has been the case for the last hundred years, at least. As each new wave of mass media has swept across American mass culture—film, radio, television, the Internet—education policymakers, philanthropists, and corporate marketeers have been eager to have it wash over the schoolhouse, too. But the enthusiasm hasn't always lasted.

Not long after the first films were invented, they were being produced for classroom commercial and noncommercial use. As early as 1910, a 336-page *Catalogue of Educational Motion Pictures* listed over 1,000 titles that could be rented by schools. There was great optimism that film would bring change as sweeping to education as it was to our popular culture at large. Thomas Edison was a most vocal and enthusiastic promoter of this idea. In 1922, he proclaimed:

> . . . the motion picture is destined to revolutionize our educational system and . . . in a few years it will supplant largely, if not entirely, the use of textbooks. I should say that on average we get about two percent efficiency out of schoolbooks as they are written today. The education of the future, as I see it, will be conducted through the medium of the motion picture . . . where it should be possible to obtain one hundred percent efficiency. (cited in Cuban, 1986, p. 9)

This same kind of boosterism accompanied the subsequent introduction of instructional radio in the 1920s. It was heralded as the "textbook of the air." William Levenson, director of the Ohio School of the Air, predicted in 1945, "The time may come when a portable radio receiver may be as common in the classroom as is the blackboard" (Cuban, 1986, p. 19). But by the 1950s few commercial radio stations maintained their school broadcasts. During the same time, the Ford Foundation underwrote the initial use of instructional television in an effort to solve the growing teacher shortage. Soon an airplane was circling the Midwest beaming down programs to six states. The enthusiasm for it was such that by 1961, Ford had invested over $20 million in 250 school systems and 50 colleges across the country. Over the next 10 years, over $100 million had been spent by both public and private sources (Cuban, 1986, p. 28). But by the 1970s, teachers reported that they showed TV programs during only 2 to 4 percent of classroom time (Tyack & Cuban, 1995, p. 123).

The 1980s and 1990s brought televised distance learning projects that used satellite, telephone, and cable technologies, as well as the desktop computer and the Internet. Education historian Larry Cuban observes (1986) that each innovation was promoted with the common conviction that technology somehow would make "instruction both productive and enriching; . . . that children somehow could learn more and faster while teachers taught less. . . . This dream has persisted from the invention of the lecture centuries ago to the early decades of this century when reformers sought efficiency through film, radio, and television" (p. 3).

However, after examining evidence of school equipment purchases and surveys of teacher usage over time, he concludes, "This rarely happened, for electronic learning was marginal to most instruction in classrooms" (Tyack & Cuban, 1995, p. 124). In many cases teachers could not get access to the equipment they needed, or the equipment was broken, or they lacked the skills to use it once they did have it. In other instances, they simply weren't able to find ways to fit the use of media into their lessons.

The Internet and digital information technologies developed in the 1990s opened up the paradigm with the promise of new ways of teaching and learning. Instead of simply giving teachers faster and even more efficient methods to deliver information to students, hypermedia tools were designed to engage students in complex self-directed inquiry projects and multilayered presentations. As education researchers Brunner and Tally (1999) document, these technologies enhanced learning in arts, science, history and language arts classes. However, they also cautioned the promise of computers and Internet technology as powerful tools for student inquiry and public conversation was realized only for some students in some schools. Significant inequities emerged along a racial and socioeconomic "digital divide" that defined access to and use of technology in schools. For those schools serving predominantly poor and working-class students, computers tended to be used in much the same way as the instructional films and television of the past: as a mechanism for instructional delivery. And so while more affluent schools provide students with inquiry-based programs that facilitate simulations for creative exploration and problem-solving, poor and working-class students are more often placed in computer labs stocked with drill and practice games, CD-ROM encyclopedias, "infotainment," and word processing software (Brunner and Tally, 1999). To bridge the digital divide, some federally funded initiatives were developed, such as the Department of Education's Community Technology Centers Program, but more resources were needed to have a significant impact in low-income schools and communities.

On the whole, though, by the late 1990s enthusiasm for the Internet as the next revolution in education began to wane even for more privileged students. Education researchers began to publicly question whether there was good evidence that computers were improving teaching and learning. Parents began to question the priorities of education administrators who were continuing to increase spending for technology at the same time they were cutting funds for libraries and arts programs. In 1997, New Jersey cut state aid to a number of school districts and then spent $10 million on classroom computers. In Union City, California, a single school district spent $27 million to buy new computer equipment for a mere 11 schools. The Kittridge Street Elementary School in Los Angeles killed its music program in 1996 to hire a technology coordinator; in Mansfield, Massachusetts, administrators dropped proposed teaching positions in art, music, and physical education and then spent $333,000 on computers; in one Virginia school the art room was turned into a computer laboratory (Oppenheimer, 1997).

Researchers in Canada have raised similar concerns. Conducting a major study of technology in the Canadian classroom, researchers from Simon Fraser University's Centre for Policy Research on Science and Technology have found that computers drain resources from basic education and require so much attention and maintenance that teachers are distracted from working with their students. The Alliance for Childhood, an international association of educators, doctors, and psychologists, suggested that the billions of dollars spent on school computers and Internet connections would be better spent on more teachers (Bailey & Vallis, 2000).

Despite the exaggerated claims that have historically been made about the power of technology in the classroom, it has made a marginal difference to instruction in most schools due to the prevalent teacher-centered pedagogy and "factory" like institutional structures. While some teachers have managed to overcome these obstacles and use technology to enhance student exploration and communication, and some federally funded efforts have sought to bridge the digital divide, this has not been the case in the majority of low-income schools and communities where unequal access to technological resources is the norm (Tyack and Cuban, 1995).

### Media Literacy

An important shift in media education took place in the early 1960s that emphasized teaching *about* the media instead of *through* the media. There was a sense that students should be encouraged to develop critical attitudes toward the media in general, and toward advertising and television in particular. Cultural critics such as Vance Packard (*The Hidden Persuaders*), Marshall McLuhan (*Understanding Media, The Gutenberg Galaxy*), and John Berger (*Ways of Seeing*) contributed to this sense, arguing for the need to move beyond the instrumental approach of using instructional media as a didactic tool. Curricula began to develop that stressed skills for analyzing television as a mass media text. The study of media-produced messages and their effects on mass audiences is the basis for what is broadly called media literacy.

A turning point in the growth of media literacy in the United States came in 1972 when the Surgeon General's Advisory Committee on Television and Social Behavior raised the connection between television violence and antisocial behavior. The following year, the Ford Foundation issued a report on children and television stating that educational institutions should be as concerned with media literacy as with language literacy. In the rush to protect children from television, the U.S. Department of Education funded critical viewing skills curricula developed at public television stations and research centers including WNET in New York and Far West Laboratories in San Francisco (Tyner, 1998). However, when funding ran out, the project did not continue, and the public policy momentum for media literacy stalled.

In contrast to the general lack of interest in media literacy in America, the 1980s were a time of great activity and development internationally. In 1981, the British Film Institute hosted a media education conference, followed the next year by an international symposium sponsored by the German Commission for UNESCO that called for comprehensive media education programs from preschool to the university level, as well as research and teacher training (German Commission for UNESCO, 1982).

Throughout the decade, media education continued to expand throughout many European nations, particularly in the United Kingdom, due to the work of grassroots organizations such as the Association for Media Education in Scotland, the Association for Media Literacy in Canada, and the Australian Teachers of Media. In some cases, such as the Canadian province of Ontario, this resulted in governmental support for media literacy as a mandated component of the school curriculum (Considine, 1990).

The theoretical and practical work of the Canadians, in addition to British media education writers such as Len Masterman, David Buckingham, and Cary Bazalgette, began to influence how media literacy was understood in the United States. When the Aspen Institute Leadership Forum on Media Literacy was held in 1992, there was great interest in learning from the codified set of practices and principles presented by media literacy colleagues from Canada. The Aspen conference was a mixed group representing arts-based media programs, community activists, university professors and researchers, the Catholic Church, and the television industry, among others. However, it lacked the participation of public school teachers and administrators, underscoring the continued separation of the media literacy field from schools in America.

To bridge the divergent perspectives represented regarding what media literacy's goals, strategies, and constituencies should be, a broad and inclusive definition was crafted: "Media literacy is the ability of a citizen to access, analyze, evaluate, and produce information for specific outcomes" (Aufderheide, 1993, p. v).

The Aspen conference sparked a new emphasis on staff development as media literacy courses and institutes for teachers were soon offered by the Harvard Graduate School of Education, Columbia University's Teachers College, New York University, Appalachian State University in North Carolina, the New Mexico State Department of Education, and Minneapolis's Walker Art Center. A few of these programs have continued, but many were short lived (Heins & Cho, 2002).

While many of the initiatives from abroad were teacher-led, the American efforts that followed in the 1990s tended to come less from the grassroots than from government and private agencies. Among the agencies and organizations that played an active role were the National Drug Control Policy and the Center for Substance Abuse Prevention, parishes of the Catholic Church, lobby organizations for regulation of children's TV such as the Center for Media Education in Washington, and medical practitioners such as the American Psychological Association and the American Academy of Pediatrics (Tyner, 1998).

In an effort to bring more grassroots teacher participation to the media education field, particularly those working in school reform, the Educational Video Center joined forces with the Annenberg Institute for School Reform to co-sponsor a national conference at the Wingspread Conference Center, ambitiously called "Media, School Reform, and the Education of All American Children." The stated purpose of the 1995 conference was "to explore how the emerging practices and principles of media education can inform serious school reform efforts underway throughout the United States. . . . We are bringing together a select group of thirty-five colleagues at this time because we believe the current climate demands that the media and school reform communities find common ground on which to work" (Wingspread Conference invitation letter, July 5, 1995).

Even though such efforts were made at finding common ground, media literacy had little impact on most of the new models of education that national school reform networks were designing. Educational associations such as the National Council of Teachers of English (which has a commission on media) and the Speech Communication Association advocated for media literacy, but the subject has failed to become a priority for most professional educational associations. This was not the case for commercial interests within the broadcast and cable television industry. Cablevision, CNN, and Channel One all have well-developed media literacy programs designed to teach students to become smarter consumers of (their own) media.

In spite of the lack of institutional support, there have been some recent developments that show progress is possible. A limited number of private schools has managed to integrate media literacy into the curriculum, as well as some public school model initiatives such as the Baltimore school district's Maryland Media Education Laboratory.

Another sign of progress on the federal level has been the multiyear collaboration between the National Endowment for the Arts and the U.S. Department of Education's Arts in Education Program. Launched by the two agencies in 2000, this marked the first time that they had ever collaborated on a media arts and media literacy initiative. By funding media literacy projects in low-income districts nationally, it showed recognition of the need for students to critically study the mass media, and of the need to bring media analysis and media arts production together. But as promising as these developments may be, it is important to keep in mind that they are still very much the exception, and are unlikely to grow to any scale given their lack of coherence as a field of study and the factory system that still determines the way the vast majority of schools are structured.

### Community Media Arts

While media literacy and community media production have mostly traveled divergent paths across the field of media education, they share some common roots in the 1960s. Early independent media artists were also influenced by the insights of theorists such as Marshall McLuhan and Buckminster Fuller, as well as by the European cinema and the American avant-garde film movements of the late 1950s and early 1960s. But while film studies and media literacy later became more the province of academia or government policymakers, the media arts found a home in the community. This was largely due to the establishment of government arts funding agencies, such as the New York State Council on the Arts in 1960, and the National Endowment for the Arts and arts councils in all 50 states by mid-decade, which institutionalized public participation in media production and film appreciation. These agencies supported the establishment of nonprofit media arts centers that provided access and training to underserved communities across the country. As film and then video became increasingly portable and inexpensive, artists and "guerilla video" antiwar activists experimented with these new technologies as tools for cultural and social change in the hope that they could create a more democratic alternative to the commercial television and film industries.

By the mid-1960s, the first 16-millimeter film production workshops for inner-city teenagers were sponsored by Channel of Soul in Buffalo and the Film Club in New York City. The Young Filmmakers' Movie Bus toured New York City setting up screenings of youth-produced projects along the route (Silverfine, 1994). As the success of these informal community-based workshops spread, so did the notion of students as makers of their own media. Bound up in the student counterculture and free speech movements of the times, this notion challenged the didactic, sender-receiver approach to learning and expression that was so pervasive in schools.

By the mid-1970s, as these movements dissipated, so did many of the first wave of video collectives that had sprung up out of them in the 1960s and early 1970s. Those that survived began to pay more serious attention to schools as recession-era school budgets were slashed and all arts programs were removed. Groups in New York City such as Downtown Community TV Center, Global Village, and Young Filmmakers provided access and training services that made it possible for students to produce their own video work. But for the most part, this training took place off-site in community-based educational settings and was never integrated into the day-to-day curricula of most schools.

By the early 1980s, the increasing availability of low-cost, high-quality equipment led to the boom in the consumer video market. This trend, along with the rapid growth of the industrial media and cable television industries, led to a greater tendency to channel students into vocational training programs at the high school and college levels. The portable handheld video camera was increasingly replaced by the camera locked down on the tripod. Instead of taking the camera into the community, students read daily school news reports from within the school studio, imitating, or in some cases parodying, the dominant model of the commercial television nightly news. The promise of youth and community empowerment was overshadowed by the promise of jobs in the industry.

Shifts in funding priorities from some foundations helped to create renewed interest in and support for community-based youth media in the 1990s. Perhaps this change was prompted by highly publicized incidents of student shootings in schools, or by the highly publicized incidents of police violence against black and Latino youth. Support from the John D. and Catherine T. MacArthur Foundation and the George Soros-funded Open Society Institute, among others, stimulated rapid growth in community-based media projects for teens across a range of cultural venues and media outlets. New organizations emerged, including Video Machete and Street Level Video in Chicago, Global Action Project and Listen Up! in New York City, and Youth Radio and Youth Outlook (YO!) in the San Francisco Bay area, to name only a few. The social consciousness and artistic experimentation of the guerrilla video era could be seen in youth activist videos produced about police brutality, sexual identity, and youth culture "happenings" such as poetry "slams." Youth-produced video programs were broadcast locally on cable access stations and nationally on PBS; youth-produced radio programs found outlets on neighborhood micro radio stations as well as on National Public Radio. New York City museums such as the Whitney Museum, the Brooklyn Museum, and the New Museum began including youth works in their own established exhibitions and even dedicated entire shows to youth media. In its 2000 national conference, the National Alliance for Media Arts and Culture featured a Youth Track especially devoted to youth media issues for the first time, and a year later hosted a month-long salon on the Internet, joined by 118 media arts practitioners, to explore the general theme of "youth making media, making movies" (Haeberle, 2001, p. 1). In the field of community arts and culture, it seemed that the idea of youth media had truly arrived and was finding expression through every form possible: video, radio, photography, newspapers, and newly emerging web-based media.

Still, even with all the growth and creative energy being generated through these arts and community-based initiatives, schools remained virtually impervious to change. Youth media really was, and continues to be, a movement that is nurtured and sustained by nonschool institutions. Unfortunately, none of the three main strands of media education—technology integration, media literacy, and community media arts production—have succeeded in penetrating the classroom or changing the system of schooling in pervasive and enduring ways.

## WORKING TOWARD SYNTHESIS AT EVC

The Educational Video Center has worked to synthesize the best ideas and practices from these three fields, making the critical analysis of media and community-based media production fundamental to all of its work. We know that important youth media work is, and must continue to be, done in the after-school community-based arena. But public schools are where the masses of kids are, and we are committed to reaching greater numbers of students through our work in the schools. However, taking into account the history of schools and media education in this country, EVC has actively collaborated with those in the school reform community in their efforts to redesign education. Until the factory model of schooling is radically transformed, there is little hope that engaging students in the analysis of media or in the production of community videos will ever become a meaningful part of the teaching and learning process. And so our model of work both draws upon and contributes to the practices and principles of learner-centered, constructivist education.

For example, EVC has integrated into its video workshops progressive pedagogical strategies such as the writing process and cooperative learning, as well as methods of portfolio and performance-based assessment. EVC's insistence that the students work collaboratively conducting interviews, shooting the camera, and editing their tapes borrows heavily from John Dewey's notion that students learn best through the cooperative experience of engaging in authentic work. On the other hand, we have shared with educators our method of using video as a tool to engage students in interdisciplinary projects as well as our approach to teaching the visual language of media.

Since much of this book reflects up [illegible]
dents in EVC workshops and classes, I [illegible]
the organization, its work, and the ide [illegible]
mission can be summed up simply: to us [illegible]

and multimedia projects as a means to develop the critical literacy, inquiry, and civic engagement skills of at-risk youth.

EVC grew from my own experiences first as a documentary maker working at Downtown Community TV Center and then as a video teacher at Satellite Academy, an alternative high school on New York's Lower East Side. The learning that took place in that school and the high quality of work the students produced there led me to establish EVC in 1984 to serve youth throughout New York City. From that first documentary class at Satellite Academy, EVC has grown into an organization with three main programs: a high school documentary workshop, a preprofessional paid internship program called YO-TV, and a professional development program for teachers.

### High School Documentary Workshop

The High School Documentary Workshop annually serves 60 public high school students. Students attend the workshop at EVC's facilities in Manhattan four afternoons per week for 20 weeks, earning school credit for their work, learning to research, shoot, and edit documentaries that explore a social or cultural issue of direct relevance to them. They present their final group projects at public screenings. At the end of the semester, their literacy, technical, and critical thinking skills are assessed through individual portfolio roundtables, during which they present evidence of their growth and learning.

### YO-TV (Youth Organizers TV)

Each year, EVC's YO-TV program provides an intensive opportunity for six of the most talented graduates from the High School Documentary Workshop to work for 10 months as paid interns producing a documentary for a professional client. This program provides an important head start in the transition from high school to work and college, especially for participants who are truly interested in and committed to pursuing a career in the media arts. Past YO-TV teams have produced documentaries commissioned by clients including PBS journalist Bill Moyers, the Whitney Museum of American Art, the Brooklyn Museum of Art, and the Human Rights Watch International Film Festival.

### Teacher Development

EVC is able to increase the scale of its work and indirectly reach hundreds more students each year by providing professional development to public school teachers. Through this program, EVC offers K–12 teachers two-week summer institutes, after-school multimedia courses, and weekly in-class consultations to integrate EVC's model of community video and web-based media projects into the curriculum. EVC staff help teachers broaden their repertoire to include strategies for facilitating community study projects, using a range of digital video and multimedia software applications, and developing and using portfolios to assess media-based learning.

## CLOSING THE DISCONNECT

The youth EVC serves live in predominantly low-income communities and reflect the racial and ethnic makeup of New York City. Most EVC students attend alternative high schools and often struggle with academic skills, family troubles, or worse. EVC aims for gender-balanced workshop participation; however, the percentage of males and females varies from semester to semester.

EVC workshop participants have produced over 100 documentaries on a range of adolescent and community issues including educational equity, media and youth identity, gun violence, AIDS, and environmental pollution. Most recently, students have produced works about the treatment of immigrant teenagers in the post-September 11 political climate. They have been broadcast on cable and network television programs, screened at venues such as Lincoln Center and the Donnell Media Center, and have won over 100 national and international festival awards, including the National Academy of Television Arts and Sciences New York Area Emmy Award.

I have seen over the years that EVC's video workshop is often a life-changing experience for the youth who participate in it. Conversations with the teens, parents, and teachers involved consistently reveal how, through EVC, inner-city students have developed a much greater sense of their potential and an increased self-confidence in their skills. For many, EVC opened up new possibilities for learning and work. Hundreds of EVC graduates have gone on to college, and many have found work in media-related jobs including network television and cable access stations, editing houses, streaming video companies, public television documentary series, and web site design firms.

The impact that the *process* of EVC's workshops has on the individual youth participants magnifies a thousandfold when the *products*—EVC's library of youth-produced documentaries—are distributed and seen by thousands of other at-risk youth across the country. These screenings serve as springboards for discussion of the documentaries and further inquiry into the issues they have raised.

This book explores some of the reasons why EVC has had such success in positively affecting the lives of students, teachers, and parents, as well as some of the challenges EVC educators face in doing this work. It takes a closer look at the role of teens and youth culture in our society, arguing for the need to develop a deeper and broader understanding of literacy in the context of that role. Specifically, Chapter 1 discusses the contradictions that shape how inner-city teenagers are portrayed in our culture as criminals by our juvenile justice system, and as trendsetters and consumers by our commercial media culture—and then explores how an expanded understanding of literacy and the language gap for children and teenagers can give them a voice to represent themselves. Chapter 2 presents a case study on teaching critical literacy at EVC. This section offers a behind-the-scenes view of a semester-long documentary workshop project about inner-city youth and guns, highlighting the ways in which students were affected by the process of creating the documentary. Chapter 3 describes what it looks like when the Teacher Development program brings EVC's methodology into a classroom setting. Through an extended case study, I use transcripts from video I recorded to give a detailed look at how the students in one alternative high school class responded deeply to the documentary making process as a means to better understand the personal issues of teen depression and suicide. Chapter 4, the conclusion, takes the argument one step further, discussing the role that after-school programs can play in increasing youth engagement and community activism through video production. I then explore institutional barriers in today's schools as well as opportunities for media education created through strategic partnerships among schools, after-school programs, and community development efforts. This convergence of fields offers important possibilities for urban youth to use media as a critical lens for seeing, learning about, and changing the world in new and powerful ways.

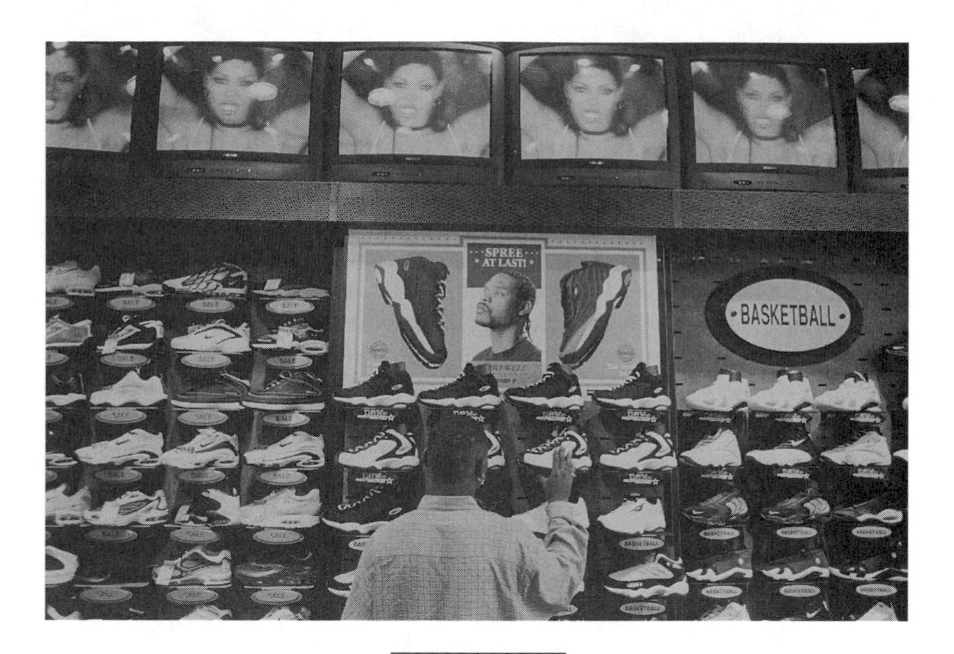


# CHAPTER 1

## *Framing the Inner-City Teenager: Criminals, Consumers, and the Literacy Gap*

AT THE EDUCATIONAL VIDEO CENTER (EVC), the documentary workshop students spend several days each term deciding what topic they will explore. We have an elaborate process of brainstorming, writing, then discussing and winnowing ideas until the students reach consensus on a subject that they feel strongly about, want to know more about, and want to inform their peers and others about. Through the process, the teens talk and write a great deal about the things that concern them most.

As we've run these sessions over the years, I've noticed that certain clusters of topics are named each time. They are neatly summarized by a recurrent choice the kids often end up facing, in some variation or other: "Should we make our tape about police brutality and youth crime or about how to become a hip-hop star?" The first cluster of topics—police–youth relations, unfair school policies, youth crime and violence, the prison system—describes the urban social world as it is for these kids, and how it is a constant source of frustration and sometimes anger. The second cluster of topics—the music and fashion industries, youth styles and trends, making it as a hip-hop artist or as an entertainment mogul—describes the social world as they wish it to be or a pleasurable escape from mundane invisibility.

We work with the teens to develop these topics further, so that they have depth and scope for themselves and viewers; and so teens have actually produced videos on a tremendous variety of topics at EVC. But the duality of frustration with official power, and attraction to mass media fantasy persists, in their daily lives, in their talk, and in their imaginations. The more time I have spent with these young people the more I have come to believe that this duality is deeply rooted in the two systems of social authority that dominate their lives.

## TWO SYSTEMS OF AUTHORITY

The teenage years are for most kids a time of rebellion and defiance. Breaking the rules of authority and pushing the limits of independence are all part of the journey from adolescence to adulthood. This journey can be especially grueling for low-income minority youth, who are far more likely than others to also face tough "adult" problems such as teen parenthood, gang violence, homelessness, incarceration, and family drug or alcohol addictions. They can neither rely on family financial resources and social support networks as their more affluent peers do, nor count on inner-city schools and social welfare agencies to seriously address their problems. As their condition of poverty and powerlessness grows with them into young adulthood, so do their feelings of despair, alienation, and anger. Our society has generally responded to inner-city teenagers in two ways: to punish them more harshly—whether in the classroom, community, or courtroom—than any other demographic group, and to market their urban youth culture more pervasively.

Two systems of authority have come to play a dominant but contradictory role in monitoring and shaping the daily life of urban youth of color in 21st-century America: the traditional social institutions, such as the police, courts, and schools, and the relatively new institutions of mass media culture, such as the music, fashion, television, and advertising industries. While the traditional system spins out its own narrative of how teenagers should and shouldn't look, think, and act in the world, the media-based popular culture spins out quite another. The former seeks to maximize social control by constructing African American and Latino teenagers as criminals and superpredators, and then punishing their acts of defiance. The latter seeks to maximize profits by naming them as hip-hop performers and trendsetters, and then co-opting their culture of defiance. The marketing and advertising media, as well as teen movies, disproportionately frame them in this way. Both systems work to silence them and deny them the intellectual and social tools of literacy that would enable them to speak for and represent themselves. Instead, physically confined in prisons, inner-city kids are rendered voiceless and invisible to the outside world. Digitally captured, their sounds and images of commercially packaged rage are sold everywhere.

## AND JUSTICE FOR SOME

Whether coercive or persuasive, both voices of authority contribute to the general criminalization of urban youth as a social fact and as a cultural phenomenon. The criminalization of urban youth of color is evident in the harsh and unequal treatment they receive in school and at every stage of the juvenile justice system. Minority teens are more likely than others to first become enmeshed in the juvenile justice system, and teens processed in urban jurisdictions receive markedly more severe outcomes than kids in suburban or rural areas (Sickmund & Snyder, 1999). A black male born in 1991 has a 29 percent chance of being imprisoned at some point in his life, compared to a 4 percent chance for a white male born that year (Beck & Bonczar, 1997).

Sometimes it seems as if the system is intentionally organized to process teenagers through overcrowded urban schools and directly into overcrowded juvenile detention facilities. Increasingly, urban high schools are taking on the look and feel of prisons: students are checked for weapons at the door by metal detectors and armed police officers, and surveillance cameras and roving guards monitor their behavior as they are locked inside for the rest of the day. School suspensions often serve as the starting point for a downward spiral into the juvenile justice system. Zero tolerance policies have resulted in African Americans being 2.6 percent times more likely to be suspended than white youth (Justice Policy Institute press release, August 29, 2001).

African American youth with no prior record are now nine times as likely as white youth to be incarcerated for a violent crime. For drug offenses, a black teen is 48 times as likely to get prison time as a white youth (Poe-Yamagata, E. & Jones, M. A., 2000). Predictably, minority youth now make up two-thirds of the over 100,000 youth confined in local detention and state correctional systems, but only comprise one-third of the adolescent population in the United States.

## SELLING TEEN REBELLION

Our popular culture's infatuation with the delinquent teenager can be traced back to such 1950s movies as *Rebel Without a Cause* and *The Wild One* that depicted the turbulent lives of antisocial teenagers in those years. An ad for *Rebel Without a Cause* boldly proclaimed, "Teenage terror torn from today's headlines," (Dale, 2001). Reading the surface text, these were cautionary tales teaching young audiences that breaking the rules in defiance of parents and police is a dangerous path to take that can lead to jail or even death. But more importantly, the subtext was that James Dean's and Marlon Brando's tragic but appealing characters represented the possibilities open to the new American teenager, an independent lifestyle that promised thrills, danger, and even premarital sex. Brando and Dean embodied the dark side of that way of life in the way they talked, fought, and seduced women; the fast cars and motorcycles they drove; the way they combed their hair; and the now iconic T-shirt, blue jeans, and leather jacket they wore. These movies reflected and helped to promote an image of the rebellious teenager that would later be known as "cool."

Even though black and brown teenagers were mostly invisible in these (or any) Hollywood films of the era, these films still had the beginnings of two ingredients that later became essential for contemporary media portrayals of marginalized urban youth. First, they were gripping stories that advertised a way of life for teenagers to emulate, a youth culture of alienation, rebellion, and style. Second, they fit into a broader system of commercial culture that made this way of life attainable.

By the 1950s, the rise in the legal age to work, leave school, and be independent from one's parents or guardians had stretched out the years between childhood and adulthood. Kids ages 12 to 17 had more money and time that didn't exist in earlier eras for leisure and consumption. The growing fashion, music, and automobile industries were making it possible for young people to buy an identity and participate in the youth culture and consumer market that was just coming into being in the postwar years.

Some 50 years later, it is safe to say that the youth market has truly come of age. And tapping into it has become an increasingly lucrative enterprise for corporate America. Children's spending has roughly doubled every 10 years for the past three decades, and tripled in the 1990s. Kids ages 4 to 12 spent $2.2 billion in 1968 and $4.2 billion in 1984. By 1994, the figure had climbed to $17.1 billion and only three years later reached $23.4 billion (McNeal, 1999). Teenagers spent a staggering $155 billion at the turn of the millennium. This figure climbs significantly when we factor in the strong influence that teen consumer preferences have on their parents' spending (Teenage Research Unlimited, 2000).

Teenage consumers have become so economically important not only because of their own spending power, but also because they are trendsetters for the mainstream market. In "Why Teens Are a Hot Market," marketing expert Peter Zollo writes, "There is no age group more involved with trends than teens. Not only are teens trendsetters for one another, they are also trendsetters for the population at large. Teen influence extends beyond fashion and popular culture, affecting the nation's economy in a big way" (Zollo, 1999).

According to market researchers, the most influential of all the young trendsetters is the disaffected minority teenager, particularly the urban black male. Drawing upon their street and prison experiences, they have created a raw and irreverent hip-hop culture that marketers describe as a "cultural triangle" of fashion, music, and sports. Marketing studies note that this urban youth culture has "a major impact on consumer preferences in the general market in the United States and worldwide in a wide range of industries, including apparel, footwear, soft drinks, packaged foods, personal-care products, and all facets of the entertainment industry" (Packaged Facts, 2000).

## YOUTH CULTURE SPIES

Stalking the elusive urban youth trendsetter has become an entire industry in itself. Market research firms compete for the business of companies with claims that they know best how teenagers think and feel, their habits and interests, what they want and what they crave. Market research firms such as Children's Market Services Inc. publish annual reports with titles such as *KidTrends*, *Targeting Teens*, and *The Under Five Crowd*. Packaged Facts publishes the report "*The U.S. Urban Youth Market: Targeting the Trendsetters*." On their company web site, Teen Research Unlimited describes just how thorough and far-reaching their cultural surveillance service is: "Teens are what we do. We listen to them, observe them, interact with them, follow them, track them, study them . . . One on one, in groups, on the Web, through e-mail, in the malls, over the phone, in our own specially designed teen facility. All over the country."

To effectively gather reliable data from inner-city teens, marketing firms have created teams of undercover market researchers known as "cool hunters." They are teen and twentysomething kids turned anthropologists who are paid to hang out with other kids in parks, tattoo parlors, dance clubs, video arcades, and pizza shops in constant pursuit of the next wave. These urban intelligence networks of kids serve as the eyes and ears on the street for companies such as Nike, Tommy Hilfiger, and Quincy Jones's

Qwest Records (Levine, 1997). As one California corporate marketing director described it, "We keep our edge because we live the lifestyle of our target audience. Our staff goes to nightclubs and malls to keep abreast of the trends. We know what young people want and don't"(quoted in Levine, 1997 p. 42).

And what do marketers learn from their research? Not surprisingly, they conclude that teens are generally distrustful of authorities, including corporate advertising, and that rebelliousness is cool. These lessons have informed the strategies advertisers increasingly use to target the youth market, such as plaster your brand across every possible private and public surface and moment of a kid's day; create promotional media that kids will not experience as commercials; and infuse your messages with a decidedly antiestablishment attitude. The bottom line is: make it cool, but don't let your marketing show.

To acquire the look and feel of counterculture, marketers have invented shadow companies that masquerade as hip, independent upstarts. But they are, in fact, part of such corporate behemoths as AT&T, Philip Morris, and Miller Brewing Company. Following on the success of Red Dog beer, Miller's microbrewery imitation, Philip Morris (the parent company of Miller) created the brand Dave's. The appeal of the new brand is the coolness of Dave, a Ben-and-Jerry type of small tobacco farmer with a yellow 1957 pickup truck who, according to Phillip Morris promotional materials as quoted in *Advertising Age*, "got fed up with cheap, fast-burning smokes. Instead of just getting mad, he did something about it . . . Dave's tobacco company was born." The claim of authenticity is an illusion. Dave doesn't exist. This story of a regular guy getting fed up with the status quo was, as a Phillip Morris spokesperson put it, "a tale of fictional imagery" (Barry, 1996).

Another trend is to create pseudo-events to advertise a particular soft drink, clothing line, or recording label and use the teen participants as the unwitting actors to help sell them. So, for example, a company pays kids to show up at a kickoff party for the new web site of one of their products, where they are entertained by a popular hip-hop band. The party is taped and promoted as a hip-hop concert sponsored by the company for audiences on TV music channels. It is then recycled as news on entertainment programs and gossip columns. The new product gets promoted, the hip-hop band and record label get promoted, the company gets to be known as a cool brand, and the kids are what make it all seem authentic, spontaneous expressions of urban youth culture (The Merchants of Cool, Frontline, 2001). The products, music, and styles being sold are effectively woven into the fabric of life so that they no longer can be identified as commercials. They are simply a part of everyday life.

And so goes the culture of consumption courting game. Market researchers send out culture spies to study the young consumers, hoping to learn how to convince them of what they should crave. The young consumers play hard to get, resisting, in their media-savvy way, these ever more sophisticated advances. Once the marketers discover cool, they force it to change into something else. The teens drive themselves to extremes to create new spaces in which to be themselves. But each time teenagers create their own unprocessed expressions of pleasure and angst—such as rock, heavy metal, punk, rap, and hip-hop—these expressions are appropriated and sold back to them in the malls as products to consume. The commercial machine they think they're escaping is always right behind them, ready to sell them the next new rendition of cool.

## EMPOWERED TO SPEAK FOR THEMSELVES

Behind the tracking, targeting, and hunting of inner-city kids as criminals and consumers is the power of language. It is their relative silence in our society, their lack of access to the tools of literacy and mass communication, that makes such framing possible. The print and visual language that is used to name these kids and the world they inhabit can build public consent for these social and economic practices, or opposition to them. For example, the mass media's "if it bleeds, it leads" approach to the news has reported stories on youth violence far out of proportion to their actual rate of occurrence. According to the Center on Media and Public Affairs, as the national homicide rate (for youth and adults) fell 20 percent between 1992 and 1996, coverage of youth homicide increased by 721 percent on all three television network news programs (We Interrupt This Message, Youthforce, 2000, p. 1).

Aside from cheapening the quality of our public discourse, the constant repetition of the same story can reinforce or perhaps construct the public's negative attitudes toward teenagers. Despite the 33 percent drop in juvenile crime since 1993, two-thirds of the American public believes that juvenile crime is still rising (We Interrupt This Message, Youthforce 2000, p. 1).

The news media have generally portrayed poor and minority youth as a problem to fix or control, a deficit to fill, a set of behaviors to prevent that puts "mainstream" society at risk. Although some school and after-school reformers promote the notion of youth as part of the solution instead of the problem, too many schools, youth programs, and social service and funding agencies still borrow from this dominant discourse. One indication of this is how often funding for at-risk youth programs is driven by violence and delinquency prevention initiatives through the Department of Justice. Education researchers noted at the start of the most recent wave of school reform in the mid-1980s, "Much of the impetus for instituting a variety of [alternative] schooling options came from widespread concerns about discipline problems and victimization in American secondary schools . . . schools with high drop out and truancy rates also have high rates of student disorder and discipline problems . . ." (McDill, Natriello, & Pallas, 1986, p. 127).

Not only does it matter how teenagers are named, it matters who does the naming. Speaking for themselves about their own lived experiences, inner-city youth offer an important alternative outside the dominant frame of consumption and crime. Their observations and insights can serve to challenge adult perceptions of teens as hostile and threatening, and also bring diversity to the voices informing public policy (Cahill, 1997).

However, to be able to understand the issues that impact their daily lives and to publicly articulate their thoughts about them—that is, to participate in civic dialogue—youth first need to have a strong grasp of language in all of its modes. Clearly, one of the main forces of education in our society, the commercial media, has little incentive to educate its young audiences about such things. Its business imperatives demand that it teach urban youth to preoccupy themselves with the consumption of what it is selling to them—the cultural triangle of fashion, music, and sports—and not necessarily to think critically and express themselves articulately about their experience of inner-city life. That job, in theory, falls to the other system of education: our public schools.

But despite decades of efforts to improve the literacy skills and learning opportunities for low-income and minority children, schools across the country have made little progress. Sadly, those students from the most impoverished communities who are most in need of a rigorous and empowering education are also those who are most poorly served by our schools. Though often highly correlated, demographics of class and race should be measured separately in educational attainment but rarely are. The national high school graduation rate was only 56 percent for African American students and 54 percent for Latino students in 1998 (Greene, 2002). While 30 of every 100 white kindergartners go on to graduate from college, only 16 of every 100 African American kindergarteners do (Borja, 2001). It seems that while the media have succeeded in teaching kids its language of images for increased consumption, schools have widely failed to teach them print literacy in preparation for work and citizenship. And the students, their families, and communities are struggling with the consequences of this language gap.

The gap in educational achievement between middle-class white students and low-income minority students begins before they even enter school and only grows over time (Hirsh, 2001). It is the underdevelopment of inner-city black and Latino children's literacy skills that is the heart of the problem (Hirsh, 2001). Most fourth graders in big-city schools can't read and understand a simple children's book (Annie E. Casey Foundation, 1999).

The challenge still remains for our nation's schools and after-school programs to effectively teach all students, including low-income black and Hispanic teens, to be fully literate and engaged citizens. The failure to meet this challenge perpetuates the marginalization of minorities and the poor in our public education system and in society at large.

To fully face this challenge requires the teaching of literacy in a way that organically links the students' development of language with the honest exploration of the contemporary world around them in all its aspects, including their treatment at the hands of the criminal justice system and the media culture industries. As producers, authors, and artists fluent in multiple literacies, inner-city youth can frame their own place in society. To practice such a pedagogy calls for a rethinking of how we teach, and understand, the notion of literacy.

## MULTIPLE LITERACIES: READING AND WRITING THE MEDIA

### The Language Gap

Researchers and policymakers have generally agreed that the literacy problems that inner-city teenagers face in high school are rooted in difficulties they have had much earlier in school, even before they started kindergarten. Some say that the language gap starts in the home and that if it is not closed by third grade, the child will have fallen too far behind to catch up. To better understand teenage learners, we need to take a closer look at the literacy problems elementary school children face in school, and the growing role of media and technology in their homes.

In writing about news reports of a growing gap in reading achievement between middle-class and low-income students, E. D. Hirsh Jr. asks why this is news; such findings, he says, have been documented for the last 50 years. Following the conclusions of the 1966 Coleman Report, Hirsh argues that the socioeconomic status of a child's family is a more important predictor of academic achievement than the school he or she attends. "Many a low-income child entering kindergarten has heard only half the words and can understand only half the meanings and language conventions of a high-income child" (Hirsh, 2001, p. 6).

Hirsh goes on to estimate that a person needs to know about 95 percent of the words he or she hears or reads in order to understand language. The other 5 percent of word meanings he or she can infer from context. So the advantaged child will routinely gain knowledge and pick up the additional 5 percent of new word meanings from a teacher's remarks. The disadvantaged child, on the other hand, "fails to gain knowledge from the exposition and also fails to learn new word meaning from the context. And to intensify that double loss, the child loses even that which he hath—his interest, self-confidence and motivation to learn" (Hirsh, 2001, p. 7).

Produced by our society's persistent inequities of race, ethnicity, and class, this language gap can only be closed, according to Hirsh, if the current emphasis on "natural development" and "creative imagination" is replaced by the more direct and explicit teaching of history, science, and vocabulary. In other words, to make up for lost time, poor kids need more teacher-directed drill-and-practice vocabulary-building exercises and plenty of tests to make sure they have memorized the words and met the standards. Thus the language gap will be closed.

This has become a common, if not predominant, argument in American education. Both schools and after-school programs are increasingly following the mantra of teach-to-the-test as they redouble their efforts to raise standardized reading and writing test scores. However, this approach to literacy and learning risks causing low income urban students to become even more detached and disengaged from school, because it widens the disconnect between what students are exposed to out of school and what they are force-fed in school.

Vocabulary, like all elements of language, is inextricably bound up in the culture, class, and community that produces and uses it. And communities use written, visual, and oral forms of language for different purposes. To insist, for example, that a child from a mountain community memorize lists of words that any kid from coastal Maine would know, such as *dinghy, dragger,* or *weir,* would be an inefficient and frustrating exercise for both student and teacher. Likewise, a city kid who has never spent time in the mountains would likely have no context for really understanding what is meant by *fuel breaks, snags,* or *slash piles*. For a low income city kid, the lack of context would be even more extreme: not being able to imagine ever leaving the city, ever needing to use fuel breaks, the inner-city kid would never see the need to remember what a fuel break is.

The upshot is that education needs to be built on intellectual and emotional scaffolds; one's sense of entitlement to intellectually and physically travel across different worlds must come into play. Hirsh's drill-and-practice vocabulary exercises mean well, but they fail to take into account the limitations—or limitlessness—of possibility that a child has experienced—and that he can imagine he will ever experience.

To be clear: the ongoing development of a student's vocabulary is an important and altogether essential intellectual tool necessary for lifelong learning. But the vocabulary of public school is the vocabulary of the white middle class. It is decontextualized and print-based, while in their nonschool hours urban children of color are immersed in the predominantly visual language of the commercial media and the predominantly oral culture of their (nonwhite, non-middle class) homes and communities. Designed to make up for lost time, the curriculum, instruction, and socialization practiced in school are altogether separate from, and in opposition to, the culture and community of a school's poorest students.

Hirsh does acknowledge that a child's family environment plays a critical role in shaping her language skills and competencies. But this acknowledgment only goes as far as to brand low-income parents' ways of speaking and being as a deficit, an obstacle to reject and overcome. The implication for children labeled "non-mainstream" is that time spent at home with the family is wasted time.

Urban students' language use needs to be valued on its own terms as one of a range of ways of communicating, and not treated as deviant or as something emanating from "the other," as the African American community-based dialect often is treated. Linguist James Paul Gee writes that "Non standard dialects and standard ones often serve different purposes, the former often signaling identification with a local, often non-mainstream community, and the latter with a wider, pluralistic and technological society and its views of who are elite and worth emulating" (Gee, 1996, p. 10).

All kids need to have a sense of rootedness in place and time. This is especially important for children who have little or no connection to their past, because of immigration, migration, or a dysfunctional home life. Poor urban youth often fit into this category. Instead of prescribing more explicit, teacher-directed drill and practice for such youth, schools should offer more opportunities for new experiences, facilitated by teachers, outside of school, in local communities and elsewhere. Experiential learning that increases children's exposure to new people, places, and ideas is especially important because language depends on relationships. Meaning is made not only through the content of what is being said, but also through who is doing the talking. Information can be more easily understood and absorbed if there is a sense of trust and familiarity established between the speaker and listener.

Even with the depressed conditions of many poor urban neighborhoods, a student's community is a vital source of learning. Conversations with peers and adults who may look the same, or have the same accents and ways of speaking as the students, can provide rich occasions for kids to develop their vocabularies, as well as to kindle their curiosity and interest in academic subjects such as science, math, and history. Students need to be encouraged to talk with their parents, neighbors, and community leaders about a range of subjects as part of oral history interviews, surveys, maps, documentaries, and reports of all kinds.

### Dr. Seuss Goes Digital

Consider once again Hirsh's claim that reading has roots in a verbal language that is contextual and community-based. I would extend that claim to argue that reading also has roots in visual language. Sight precedes speech. A child first makes sense of the world as a patchwork of images, which incidentally are accompanied by sounds. Only much later do printed words come into play. If Hirsh and others are proposing new ways to teach literacy based on kids' preschool language experiences in the home, they are omitting a critical part of that experience: the powerful role of image and sound in electronic media.

The amount of time that preschool children generally spend every day watching, listening to, and playing with electronic media in the home has been documented (the Henry J. Kaiser Family Foundation, 1999). What is less well known is the impact these interactions have on the development of children's thinking and print literacy skills. It is a complicated question since the content and the context of those interactions are so important, as is the prior knowledge that the child uses to make sense of them. But I believe that a better understanding of kids' visual, aural, and textual experience of media in the home can help educators develop more effective strategies for teaching reading and writing in school.

While more research is needed before definitive conclusions about learning can be drawn, the evidence suggests that there is a shift under way in the relationship between author and reader, and between reader and text. Traditionally, children have learned to read primarily by having stories read aloud to them. They experience the printed word essentially as an oral performance accompanied by the book's illustrations. In these performances, the reader (often the parent) is free to interpret the author's meaning and voice and the listener (the child) is free to participate in the reading by asking questions, adding to the story, feeling the pages, having passages repeated or skipped, or even acting out parts of the story. The reading most often takes place as a part of the bedtime ritual. The aura of traditional oral storytelling is recreated to the extent that it is an interactive, social experience.

A sign of more developed literacy skills is the ability to read silently, "to yourself." This ability represents the movement from an oral to an interior experience. In this case, the reader makes sense of the writer's words privately and directly, without the mediation and social context of the oral reading. Silent reading, of course, allows for no interpretive dialogue with the storyteller, doesn't engage the aural senses, and increasingly restricts the visual senses, as more advanced books include fewer illustrations. This requires that the reader think more abstractly. He must rely more heavily on his imagination to conjure up the sensual information that is suggested by the writer's words. The interactive dialogue that takes place is between the author's printed ideas and the reader's interior voice as developed by his own particular base of knowledge and lived experience. Through this process, the reader reconstructs the images, voices, and human experience of the story.

The shift under way is occurring because television, "sound story" books, CD-ROMs, and videos all engage the young reader's visual and aural senses in reproducing the performance experience of oral storytelling. "Sound story" books give the reader literally all the bells and whistles that silent, nonelectronic books don't have. The child can experience the excitement of pressing an icon and hearing a few bars of a circus song as Dumbo the elephant arrives, the Joker's laugh as he fights Batman, or the car phone ringing in a book about a car ride. The technology and the packaging of the book are often of more interest than the contents of the story. In some cases, the lines between conventional notions of book, toy, and music box become hard to find.

Television, film, video, and CD-ROMs present children with a feast of sensory stimulation. They engage almost the full range of senses to tell their story through a complex combination of images, voices, music, sound effects, graphics, and text. And the stories are more likely to be retained by the child viewer than by the child reader because of the rich range of visual and aural information conveyed.

Needless to say, this mode of storytelling is heavily mediated. Scriptwriters, directors, producers, editors, actors, animators, composers, musicians, and sponsors all contribute to the construction of the electronic media version of the book. This team of media makers collectively takes the place of both the author and the parent reading the bedtime story. Their creation is at the same time both a text and a performance.

Literacy teachers need to take into account both the abundance and the variety of non-print stories their students "read" from pre-school through high school. Educators must apply a broad knowledge of language, media, technology, and culture to their teaching since their students use multiple literacies to make sense of these various media—literacies that are constructed by variables such as race, class, ethnicity, gender, and age. The problem is the serious imbalance that exists for inner-city kids between their relatively strong command of oral and visual language for use in their local community and in the commercial media environment, and their weak grasp of the print-based language they need to succeed in school, and later in the world of work.

Bringing a deeper understanding of those languages, in all their richness and complexity, to the process of teaching and learning might just go a long way toward overcoming this imbalance and bridging the language gap. Doing so will enable marginalized teenagers to make it through their difficult journey into adulthood, fully able to speak, represent, and demand recognition for themselves and their community.

## CHAPTER 2

# *Cameras and Guns in the Streets: Teaching Critical Literacy in the Documentary Workshop*

EACH SEMESTER, THE EDUCATIONAL VIDEO CENTER runs a program called the High School Documentary Workshop, engaging teams of students in a sustained video-based inquiry into a social issue in their community. The workshop—Doc Workshop, as it's called—gives students an opportunity to voice the ideas, questions, and possible solutions they might have about difficult issues that affect them on both a deep, personal level and a larger, systemic level. Through this community-based approach to media education, students routinely use visual, aural, and print modes of communication in their daily work. Students learn to pose their own questions and search for answers to them over the course of their project. The documentary-making process opens up all sorts of new possibilities for teaching critical literacy skills. Those new possibilities have implications for bridging the in-school/out-of-school disconnect that urban youth are so often subject to, along with implications for closing the literacy gap described in the previous chapters.

For as many possibilities as the workshop opens up, however, it also raises plenty of challenges. The students who come to EVC typically have poor records of academic achievement, have had little if any prior experience making videos, and certainly have never before conducted social research in the community. They tend to experience school as a place that created more barriers than bridges between the print-based language they learned in school and the oral culture they learned during their nonschool hours at home, in their community, and from the mass media.

The students' families' low-income/low-vocabulary status, as discussed in the previous chapter, is a good predictor of their underdeveloped reading, writing, and critical thinking skills. Most of the kids are far more fluent in spoken language than in written, have little experience using libraries, and are often suspicious of information generated by sources outside their local neighborhood. Engaging these students in a social documentary research project raises a number of questions and problems regarding the teaching of research and literacy skills to marginalized students.

In this chapter, I follow a team of high school students who spent a semester at EVC creating a documentary, which they called *Young Gunz*, about the problem of gun violence among urban teenagers. With the abovementioned possibilities and challenges in mind, I explore how oral culture, visual language, and the experience of growing up in economically depressed communities shape the way these kids learn to bring a critical literacy to the way they make sense of and act upon the world around them.

Interviews and observations of the students at work illustrate how the Doc Workshop helps to transform students' feelings of hopelessness into active community engagement. I believe that these young video makers have important lessons to teach us about how to more effectively use media technologies and cultural traditions to build upon students' skills of visual and oral expression as stepping-stones, instead of stumbling blocks, to learning.

## THE DOC WORKSHOP

The Doc Workshop was organized around a few basic practices and principles.

- Through the process of creating their documentary project, the students choose to explore what are for them the important questions and problems they face in their communities, schools, and homes. Their communities are a rich source of information to use in their inquiry.

- The projects are inclusive: every student regardless of his or her past record of academic achievement can contribute ideas and talents in a meaningful way as an illustrator, animator, camera operator, editor, sound technician, interviewer, poet, musician, actor, writer, or researcher.
- The documentary production process is sustained and collaborative. Students work in teams of about 12 for the duration of an 18-week semester. They collaborate on all the stages of production, from choosing the topic to presenting the finished tape, and experience a variety of roles throughout the project.
- The critical analysis of media is integrated throughout the documentary production process. Students deconstruct a range of media including still images, commercials, narrative films, and professional and youth-produced documentaries to understand how the language of media can be used to communicate messages and tell stories.
- The youth producers present their finished documentary to public audiences who will critique, appreciate, and sometimes use the students' tape in their own community.
- The students present drafts of their video and written work in portfolio roundtables as evidence of their intellectual and artistic development. Parents, teachers, peers, media professionals, and other members of the community participate in the assessment of their learning.

The Doc Workshop students who worked on the *Young Gunz* project chose to make their tape about the problem of gun violence because it was such a pervasive problem in their lives. There were 12 high school students in the crew, and eight of them reported that a friend or family member had recently died a gun-related death. As part of the production process, the students interviewed each other and talked to teenagers in the streets and housing projects of the community, who told harrowing stories of young lives crippled or lost to senseless gun violence. They recorded their own poetry readings, enacted skits, and edited a montage of violent images from the media including westerns, war movies, and video games.

But as was the case with other student teams, the *Young Gunz* crew didn't know how to practice traditional methods of research for their tape. That is, they did not pose a problem and then gather, evaluate, and synthesize information from a range of sources to make a reasoned argument for some action to be taken. Their tape included no statements from academics and government experts; no references to foundation reports, books, news articles; nor other such evidence that could support their arguments. They did give some basic explanations about the causes of and possible solutions to youth gun violence, but these were largely drawn from their own experiences, not from the theories or prior research of others. Sources of information were generally oral and community-based, not printed and academy-based. It seemed they learned to collect and edit compelling stories, but not to make a well-researched argument. They learned to name the problem of violence in their community, but not to suggest how it could be changed.

## OUT ON A SHOOT

After grabbing a quick lunch in their school cafeterias, the students begin packing up their book bags to leave for the day. They won't be going to any afternoon classes. Instead, they take the nearest subway from neighborhoods across New York City to the Educational Video Center's mid-Manhattan facilities. There they attend the Doc Workshop from 1:00 P.M. until 4:00 P.M.—often staying past 5:00 P.M.—and earn school credit for their work. They come because they want to learn how to use video cameras and editing equipment to express their ideas and feelings about the things that matter most deeply to them. And as each group inevitably does, at the end of each semester (after editing late into the evening for the final 10 days of the program), they manage to finish their documentary by the deadline and present it at a premiere screening.

Going out on a shoot is arguably the most essential and certainly the most exciting part of the documentary-making experience. This is when the crew takes their cameras, mics, and other gear into the community to ask questions and collect the information, stories, and images that will later be edited into their final documentary.

In most schools, the streets don't count for much as a source of information and knowledge. But for journalists and documentary makers, the streets can prove to be an invaluable source. This was certainly true for the *Young Gunz* crew. The interviews they conducted on the streets produced a rich and often unexpected array of opinions and personal stories. The following is a description and partial transcript of one of the first shoots the *Young Gunz* crew went on.

Sam nervously taps the microphone against his palm as he approaches the group of four teenagers hanging out in front of the Fort Greene, Brooklyn, projects. This is the first time he has ever conducted an interview. Joseph shifts the camera on his shoulder and zooms in on the guy wearing the open leather jacket and the silver cross hanging on his broad chest. He tries to keep the shiny cross in focus as he walks across the street behind Sam. They both later agree that these four young men are probably drug dealers. Sam introduces the video crew and teacher, Kim, takes a deep breath, and asks his first question.

"How do you feel about guns in the community?"

Without hesitation, the leather-jacketed leader of the group responds: "I feel we need *more* guns in the community."

Lina, listening through her headphones, glances down at the portable video recorder and adjusts the audio meter as it jumps too far into the red.

"Why do you feel that?" Sam asks.

"Because everyone has guns, and we have the right to bear arms and defend ourselves." A small crowd gathers around the video crew, thinking it might be the local news.

Caught up in the excitement, Sam presses on with the interview: "So you following the laws of the Constitution, then."

"No. Actually, we following the laws of the street."

This statement provokes nods of approval from the other three guys in the group and some shaking heads and murmurs of disapproval from the onlookers. LaToya, whose job on this shoot is to line up the street interviews, notices a young woman with a baby carriage who is getting visibly agitated. She asks the woman if she would be willing to give her opinion on camera. The street corner is now buzzing with conversation.

## TALKING AND WATCHING WORDS

When the students are out on a shoot, they are usually too preoccupied and excited trying to ask the right questions, point the microphone in the right direction, and keep the camera steady and in focus to be able to also think deeply about what is actually being talked about. This is natural, since they have had little or no prior experience videotaping interviews. However, the next step in the documentary production process—reviewing and logging the video footage—frees them to think more critically about the content of what they shot. A conversation that Sam and Joseph have while viewing their Fort Greene interview tapes illustrates the multiple levels of reflection that naturally take place throughout the production process:

From the taped interview they are watching:

*Sam:* "How many people do you know that own guns, or have been hurt by guns?"

*Man in leather jacket:* "Many."

*Sam:* "Don't you think its really hurtin' our community rather than doing more for it?"

*Man in leather jacket:* "It can't be hurting it too much because the police have guns and they're really hurting our community. So, I say we slaughter them."

Sam and Joseph pause the tape they are viewing and talk:

*Joseph:* "But look, they talk about, 'We need more guns to defend ourselves.' Who they using guns against? They ain't usin' 'em against the cops."
*Sam:* "They usin' 'em against both."
*Joseph:* "They usin' 'em against each other. They not using 'em against the cops."
*Sam:* "And the cops, too."
*Joseph:* "You hear about cops getting shot now. For every one cop that gets shot, how many kids, how many black kids, that's killing each other?"
*Sam:* "Oh shit, there's like . . . that's a number I can't even define."
*Joseph:* "So what he's saying don't make no sense, then."
*Sam:* "But you gotta see it from his point of view. He's a pusher."

This conversation shows how the student producers begin to distance themselves from their documentary subjects. The people they see and the problems they live with every day become visible to them as things outside their lives that can be held up to a critical light. They compare the story they have recorded to their own experiences and begin to question its truthfulness and form hypotheses of their own. To reach a verifiable conclusion to their own debate, they find that anecdotal experience is not enough. They begin to shift their social position from being a *participant in the community* to *a participant-observer of the community*.

However, it is not sufficient for the students' discussion of their taped interview to end there. A new learning opportunity emerges from this talk. They have raised important questions about youth-on-youth violence that require further research. Sam's remark that the number of African American youths who have killed each other is "a number I can't even define" can be synonymous with the word "countless," but stronger, as a description of how unfathomable and unacceptable the amount is. It can also be understood as an admission of his lack of knowledge of this fact. Instead of accepting it as an unknown and perhaps an unknowable number, the students should make this part of their research. Here then lies the challenge for the teacher: to both expand the students' capacity for multiple literacies and deepen their critical character. We will return to this challenge later in the chapter, exploring some of the intellectual and cultural reasons why many students have such difficulty with reading and research.

## SELF-PORTRAITS

In addition to gathering information and stories from other people, the student producers also add their own perspectives to the mix. After all, giving the students an opportunity to express their ideas, questions, and concerns is at the heart of what the Doc Workshop is all about. So the student videographers end up in some way being both documenters and documented; there is an element of self-reflection or self-portrait in every project. Interviewing their friends, family members, and each other enables them to bring both an outsider's and an insider's perspective to the issues they explore. This opens up tremendous opportunities for the students, but it also creates some problems.

In the case of the *Young Gunz* project, to investigate the subject of teenagers and guns often meant investigating their friends. And asking the wrong questions, or in some cases asking any questions, went against the unspoken rules of the streets. As Luis explains, "The rule is, you mind your own business. I don't know why it's a rule. But it's been a rule since before I was born. For instance, I would never go and tell the cops about the drug dealers that I know. If I were to snitch on the drug dealers, I'd lose my respect and probably my life as well."

Having students turn the cameras on themselves was particularly difficult since it could have meant revealing potentially incriminating secrets to the public or, worse, to their parents. But even more complicated was what a self-directed inquiry process meant to their own sense of self. Examining one's own conditions of daily life often turns "givens" into questions or problems. And posing something as a problem implies a search for solutions. As most students explained, there were no solutions to gun violence. Change was just not an option worth considering. All of their experiences at home, in school, and in the neighborhood taught them that nothing ever changed, nor could they even imagine the remotest possibility of change.

An example of this is the moving testimonial at the end of the tape that crew member Luis gives to his fallen brother-in-law:

> It was over nothing. Defending the honor of my sister. That's what it was over. And he wound up getting killed. Friends drew a memorial on the streets where he laid. And my older sister Wanda became a widow. What hurt everyone the most, was that

> Raymond would never be able to know his unborn son, Raymond Jr. And Raymond Jr. would never be able to know firsthand what a great man his father was.

Luis wanted to publicly mourn the loss of his brother-in-law, to bear witness to the reality of life in his neighborhood. But when he was pressed for possible solutions to the problem, he repeatedly insisted that there are none.

The EVC students seemed to be, as philosopher Maxine Greene described so well, "sunk in the everydayness" of life. While they clearly felt the weight of the social order, they could not fully name or resist it. They felt conditioned, determined, even fated by prevailing circumstances, and so perceived the violence and inequity that surrounded them as wholly normal, as predictable as natural laws (Greene, 1988, p. 124). They suffered from what Dewey called the "anesthetic" in experience that numbs people into an inability to imagine the existence of, much less search for, alternatives (Dewey, 1934).

So for a variety of reasons, telling one's own story was both an empowering and potentially dangerous act. Instead of simply turning the camera on themselves, the students often felt more comfortable turning them on their friends, neighbors, and family members. Occasionally, they interviewed each other or told their own stories in the form of narration or autobiographical poetry read over images of themselves.

For example, there was talk in the group that Erika had done some pretty bad things when she was in a gang down South. She was no stranger to guns and had beat up some people for money. Erika also spent time in the Spofford juvenile detention facility. She claimed that she was now through with guns, although she spent most of her time with a boyfriend who carried one. Erika was a potentially valuable resource to the group, as they were searching for someone to talk on camera about personal experiences with guns. But she was living with her mother again, after some time apart, and was worried that her mother would learn through the video about the details of her past life.

Erika avoided the issue and then said, "Why everybody keep bringing that up? You know, I said one little thing, everybody keep bringing that up! I'm a thug now. It wasn't all that . . . All right! I used to beat people up! You know what I'm sayin'? I used to beat people up for a little cream here and there. I ain't no Queen Latifah of this piece, I aint no Cleo." (Cleo, played by rapper/actress Queen Latifah, was the bank robber heroine of the movie *Set It Off*.)

It wasn't until the final weeks of the semester that Erika felt safe enough to open a part of her private world to the inquiring eye of the camera. She brought a camera home with her and shot interviews with her boyfriend and his cousin. Pulling a large gun out of his pants, he says, "This is what I carry. This is a .44 Magnum. This is one of the most powerful handguns in the world. You know what I'm saying?"

She also talked about her past involvement in a youth gang and described her attraction to guns in a segment of the documentary's narration: "I used to like holding guns. The power, how they looked, shooting them off . . ." She was self-reflective in so far as she knew she had "been through a lot of stuff" as she told her story of violence and loss (for this book but not for her documentary):

> Me being 18, I think I've been through a lot of stuff that 18 year old not supposed to be going through. . . . Me and my mother just starting to get close. Because I never really lived with my mother. I lived with my grandmother and my aunts, so I was never really close to my mother. My grandmother, I used to be close to her. She died, and that kind of messed me up. I started really getting into this damn stuff, this gang. Not really a gang. I say, organization. Trying to belong to somewhere else. Trying to be something I'm not. And seeing a lot of my friends die, 'cause of they trying to be something they're not. I seen two of my friends died of AIDS. I seen one of my friends die 'cause she got stabbed. I could say I seen her die in front of my face but, when she got stabbed she was alive. At the hospital she died there. She bled to death. I been through a lot of stuff. I've seen a lot of stuff. I'm not supposed to be an 18-year-old, seeing all that stuff right about now.

Her analysis was also clear as to the decision she made to make money as a gang member instead of taking a fast food restaurant–type job. "Working in a Roy Rogers. C'mon now. And people telling me, 'Clean the flo!' For a dollar. Get outa here. I'm not working for them. Not for no Yankee Man. I'm not. I'd rather sell dru—, oh shit." She stopped herself from going on, remembering she was being recorded. But when asked to reflect on her life experiences and the possibility for future change, she believed there was little if anything to be done.

## MAKING IT PUBLIC

In the end, the young documentary makers constructed a powerful collection of words, music, and images that represented their own framing of reality. They used their cameras and editing equipment to conjure a world, as they saw it, on tape. While they took no clear position as to the causes or solutions to youth gun violence, their documentation showed "the way things are," and did so with a simple truthfulness. The student poem that closes the documentary paints a dark picture of the harsh life in which so many inner-city teenagers find themselves.

*A young Black kid, from the mean streets of Brooklyn, the projects to be exact*
*Where I stand under my building, crack my gat, and sell crack*
*I smoke blunts and drink beer*
*Living life without fear*
*I go to bed at night*
*To the sound of gunfights*
*Everyday it seems as if one of my boys is gunned down*
*Around town*
*I shed a tear, spill some beer*
*And thank God I'm still here*
*If I live to be twenty-one*
*I feel as though the battle has been won*
*Not yet a high school grad, but already a high school dad*
*Because of some fun I had*
*While others are preparing for college*
*I stay busy working on my street knowledge*
*A thug inside and out*
*This is the only thing I know, this is what I'm about*
*So each night in bed as I lay*
*I pray to make it just one more day.*

Naming the way things are, the students made public their friends' as well as their own private feelings of hopelessness and fear. These feelings were certainly understandable given the personal tragedies many of them had already lived through. However, having teenagers name such conditions without also questioning how they came into being and how they can be changed risks pushing despair over the edge into fatalism. As an ahistorical project, it can turn the way things are into the way things will always be. The students then risk becoming stuck in Dewey's "anesthetic" of daily life.

While making their documentary, the students seemed captivated by the stories they heard. They couldn't help but be drawn in by the bravado of outlaws and the loss of the survivors, and by whole cycle of random death and blind vengeance. But when they screened it in public, the *Young Gunz* team was able to gain some distance and begin to take apart what they had put together. Showing their tape at libraries, schools, community centers, and video festivals meant they had to answer youth and adult audiences who wanted to know such things as why they had decided to ask a particular question or had not asked another; why they decided to make their tape in the first place; what they thought the solution was to youth violence; and what they had learned in the process. Pressed to explain and reflect on what they had created and how they might do it differently next time, the kids were given new opportunities to break the spell of the everydayness of life.

Public screenings had the power to break this spell in part because they created a contrast of realities: familiar and strange, ordinary and extraordinary. The faces up on the video monitors were of ordinary kids. They were shot against the backdrop of a familiar urban landscape: streets, subways, parks, housing projects, and even a McDonald's. These were inner-city teenagers who are so ordinary they routinely go unnoticed. But their recorded voices that filled the room were extraordinary. These voices sounded that way not because they were saying such new things. They were extraordinary because most adults hadn't really heard them before. It was startling for the youth in the audience, too, to see other kids who look and sound just like them being listened to and taken so seriously. Carried from the margins into the screening rooms of mainstream institutions, these stories of anger, confusion, and sadness reverberated in lasting ways.

It was also strange for the Doc Workshop students to be up onstage in front of adults and peers, presenting their ideas as journalists and artists and answering questions as experts. This was a role that they had never had before. Even though some claimed their thinking about gun violence hadn't changed, their *talking* about it had. That is, the crew was becoming practiced in public dialogue about public problems. They were getting used to the open and intergenerational exchange of ideas about issues in their community, and the idea that in this public conversation, their ideas and experiences really mattered. After all, their video was at the center of it all. They may not have had all the answers. But by re-presenting a slice of life as they saw it—as raw and imperfect as it may be—back to the community from which it was taken, they were posing a problem that demanded a response.

With each showing, *Young Gunz* sparked vigorous debates among the audience members that, one hopes, continued on after the screening ended. The public screenings raised the possibility for audiences of extending the students' inquiry into an ongoing endeavor shared by their parents, friends, and neighbors in the broader community. Perhaps, then, over time, a reinvigorated civic dialogue could move these young documentary makers and their audiences further along a critical and transformative process from the descriptive—"What is this experience?"—and the reactive—"How could this be?"—to the active—"How can it be otherwise?"

## TRUSTING INFORMATION

While the immediate technical and artistic goal of EVC's Doc Workshop is for students to learn to make documentaries, the educational goal is deeper and more long-term. It is to develop students' literacy and critical thinking skills so they will become lifelong, autonomous learners. Working toward this goal presents EVC teachers with a number of challenges. At the start of the Workshop, most EVC students lack the basic print literacy and research skills needed for their documentary. These problems are connected to and magnified by two general sets of beliefs and feelings that the students repeatedly expressed. First, many students say they don't trust information conveyed through the printed word. Some students claim to distrust information reported by any sources—including the electronic and print news media—other than someone in their neighborhood. Their problem of not knowing how to gather and make sense of information is therefore compounded by their difficulty in knowing how to decide what and what not to believe. And second, they often voice a deep sense of hopelessness and pessimism that any amount of learning or community involvement could make a difference in the social conditions that shape their lives. In short, they feel little motivation or reason for improving their reading, writing, or research skills.

At its most basic, the students' inquiry begins with and spirals out of the act of questioning, as all inquiry does. But for questions to eventually lead to answers—and perhaps to new questions—inquirers must learn where and how to gather information. Then they need to learn how to assess the reliability of the information they obtain, and finally how to interpret and integrate the new data into their existing frameworks of knowledge and experience. This is fundamentally a social and intellectual process, one that is about access to people and institutions just as it is also about access to ideas and information.

But for the learners at EVC, this way of knowing is limited by a number of factors, both social and intellectual. While they learned to exploit the streets as a valuable site for research, the students often perceived libraries as being generally off limits to them as far as research was concerned. In fact, the majority of the students in the *Young Gunz* group had never been to a public library before attending the Doc Workshop, although they had made it to their junior and senior years of high school. As low-income minority teenagers with underdeveloped reading and writing skills, they felt the power of the library to be quite intimidating. Their deep discomfort with reading and writing led to conflicting feelings about the value and reliability of the printed word. Some trusted print-based information simply because it was housed in a library, and others voiced a clear preference for oral communication, dismissing the whole idea of libraries. This is best illustrated through a transcript of a conversation I had with two *Young Gunz* student producers, LaToya and Hayden, at the start of their project:

*Steve:* "How do you know if the information you are getting is true?"
*LaToya:* "I went to the library. Found it out."
*Hayden:* "Library. The almighty power. You can't argue with that. That's where the teacher sends you. 'Go look it up in the library.' Hey. Whatever you find in the library most likely has to be true. If it's in there in the books and the reference books, it's true."
*Steve (to LaToya)*: "Is that what you think, too?"
*LaToya:* "Well, me personally, I wouldn't know. 'Cause I don't like going to the library. I wouldn't know. I go by word of ear. I go by word of ear."

Going by "word of ear" was not only about an oral-dominant tradition of learning through talk rather than through reading. It also implied a broader recognition of the social connections between literacy, knowledge, and class. There were those who had book knowledge and those who had knowledge gained from talk. However, the students described the connection between literacy and class not in conceptual terms, but in the more concrete categories of appearance and place. Less educated, poorer people hang out in street clothes on inner-city blocks, and more educated, wealthier people work in suits in midtown offices.

Mara, a 15-year-old member of the *Young Gunz* team, shared similar beliefs. When asked how she and her video team members gathered information, she explained, "We found out the truth. Like the street way of knowing it. Getting information the street way is better than getting it the other way, you know, like the people with the suit and tie. 'Cause they don't really know. Who really knows is the people who are on the street."

To assess the reliability of street information, according to the students, one must first assess the reliability of the source. This had everything to do with the quality of the relationship the students had with their sources. Trust came when the information could be interpersonally contextualized, that is, when it came from a friend or family member or someone else they personally knew. LaToya explained, "I learned to trust nobody that don't trust me. That's the way my mother taught me. Don't trust nobody that don't trust you."

Trust in the veracity of information could no longer be sustained once it was removed from the immediate context of personal experience. They felt they could not trust the information if the source was an unknown writer with no personal connection to them. It was not so much the message itself, but how it was delivered and who delivered it. If it was too decontextualized in terms of language and culture, then the information was suspect. This suspicion certainly applied to the information reported in the news media.

After graduating from high school, Joseph (one of the *Young Gunz* production team) assisted with this book by conducting interviews with several students who voiced skepticism and some confusion regarding the trustworthiness of the news. One of his friends, a 16-year-old sophomore from Brooklyn, doesn't trust the news to report daily events accurately. "A lot of times I'll watch the news and all they report is a half the story," he said. "For example, in my building once this guy was being harassed by the police for no reason and then a fight broke out. The guy was beaten up badly but the next day in the paper they reported that the guy instigated the whole incident when in reality he was the victim."

When asked how he knew what to trust and what not to trust on television, Hayden responded: "See, you don't. That's the thing about TV. TELL-LIES-TO-THE-VISION. You never know what to believe and what not to believe."

Erika made a distinction between the reliability of print and television news. "When you read something in a newspaper, a magazine, or a book, five out of ten, it's true. TV, it's exaggerated. It's exaggerated so you can watch it . . . I can tell when someone is lying or telling the truth. Most of the time. I don't know how I do it. I just have an instinct."

LaToya described her skepticism watching the news on television. "That's why I turn the news. If they telling me about something I don't know about and I'm not there, so why am I sitting there watching them if I don't really trust them? They could be telling me a bold-faced lie." She went on to explain how when her cousin was shot, the reporters got the story all wrong.

John, who is white and middle-class, was the one student who did trust the news. He watches the news regularly, at least the first five minutes, because as he explained, "It's the most interesting. It's always about shootings or some kind of death." He then explained that his father was a television news reporter.

## LOCAL INTERPRETERS

Students with poor literacy skills often try to avoid doing much reading, writing, or research by hiding behind cloaks of cynicism or boredom. But interviews with the EVC students indicate that they were interested in and had knowledge of political and social issues. It is just that they tended to learn about such things out of school through talk rather than reading. The teenagers noted how much they learned about contemporary and historical events from "local interpreters" such as an aunt, older brother, pastor, or friend. Such talk yielded valuable information for the students simply because of their sources' higher level of print literacy and more extensive life experiences. And above all, they were reliable and trustworthy sources.

For example, when asked how he learned about things that happened before he was born if not from books, Sam replied, "I get my information from older people that's been around this planet longer than I have. They have gotten their taste of how life was back in the days of the civil rights movement and stuff like that. All that stuff that people was involved in back then. . . . Instead they tell the younger children, the next generation, they give us the info of what went down when they was our age." When he visits his aunts, Sam explained, he learns a lot from the conversations they have about politics and history. Most recently they talked about the welfare system and how he can plan to get himself off public assistance.

Another student said that he leans on his older brother a lot to learn more about things he doesn't believe or understand. "I talk to my brother a lot because I know he won't lie to me and he'll try to help me in every way possible."

Mara also described how she relies on her family, specifically her mother, rather than the news to learn about most political and social issues. Church is another important source of information for her: "When I'm in church and my pastor is preaching, I feel very confident that what he tells me is truthful."

While the spoken word clearly plays a dominant role in these students' lives, the written word is still quite present, but in a less visible position. For example, according to Joseph, several of his friends who rarely read learned a lot about politics, history, and current events though street-corner discussions they had with one of their friends who is an avid reader. As his friend explains it, "When I read something, I like to put my boys on to what I've read so they can be aware of what's going on."

## OUT ON A SHOOT (REVISITED)

Engaging students in the planning, conducting, and review of interviews is a central part of EVC's teaching methodology. It is a successful strategy not only because it allows those students with weak reading and writing skills to contribute to the group's research process, but also because it validates and builds upon the oral traditions of the students and their community. It allows local interpreters in the community to contribute their knowledge and experience to the group inquiry. With guidance from the teacher, students can connect with community leaders and grassroots organizations working for social change. This approach aims to improve the literacy and critical thinking skills of individual students while at the same time addressing the systemic social and cultural marginalization that most inner-city students experience.

For most Doc Workshop students, going out on shoots to record interviews is an experience unlike any they have had in school. Each foray into the field is a relatively unpredictable encounter determined to a large degree by the students and the people they interview. For example, a crowd might gather and bystanders might feel compelled to add their own opinions to the interview. Advance planning and preparation are essential. But it is the chemistry of the moment and the ability to be spontaneous and squeeze the most out of that moment that counts the most. If their shoot goes well, students will have been able to draw out and record information and insights—street knowledge—that they will use to enrich their documentary.

Even if they were only mildly interested in the information they ended up capturing on tape, the experience of collecting it almost always completely engaged them. The students were excited to just be outdoors and have it count as an educational experience. Beyond that, the thrill of going out on the shoot had something to do with the fact that it broke some of the students' commonly held rules of social interaction. It also challenged certain power relations between the teenagers and the adults they interviewed, as well as between marginalized and more privileged communities.

Simply the act of walking up to complete strangers with microphone and camera in hand and asking them questions breaks students of one of the most basic rules they have grown up with: "Don't talk to strangers." Moreover, for the *Young Gunz* videographers to do this also went against the unspoken rule that youth shouldn't question authority. Principals, teachers, parents, and policemen are empowered to question teenagers, but not the other way around. The EVC students also broke with the convention practiced by traditional high school journalism classes of conducting interviews within controlled settings such as professional offices or TV studios, but not out on the streets.

It is much more common than it was even 10 years ago to see tourists with consumer video cameras taping their family trips or parents taping their children's school plays and sports events. But average citizens, and especially youth of color, are not expected to use professional-quality equipment and to be engaged in the more serious business of gathering news and producing documentaries. This is still considered to be the sole province of mainstream media institutions such as local and network television stations. It is a shift in power relations for traditionally marginalized teenagers to also do so. The youth production crew felt a shared sense that simply having cameras in their hands challenged widely held assumptions about who gets to use the means of communications in our society.

On an affective level, facilitating the group experience of going out on video shoots almost always enhanced the sense of personal accomplishment and empowerment for the student participants. On a cognitive level, teaching the youth producers interviewing skills was facilitated by their relative preference for talking and listening instead of writing. Using the interview experience, however, to further develop their research and literacy skills was hindered by the students' complete lack of prior experience conducting social research projects. The investigation of often controversial, outside-of-school social issues (such as youth violence, race relations, AIDS, and teen sexuality) is rarely if ever done in academic classrooms. Most of the students who come to EVC have never had the experience of researching social issues in the community, let alone discussing them in class. There is an institutional bias against teaching controversial social issues in school because doing so risks complaints from parents and interest groups, which then risks bad publicity in the media.

In addition, there are structural obstacles to the teaching of documentary inquiry as an academic subject in school, such as the short duration of most classes (45 minutes), which precludes leaving the building to go out on a shoot in the community; the lack of training that would prepare teachers to engage their students in such study; and the fact that the content learned from such local projects is not tested on the state-mandated standardized exams. So it is not surprising that when asked if teachers ever talked about community issues in her school classes, Lina responded:

> Not really. If we do talk about issues, it's like a one-on-one conversation with a teacher. Or a teacher is just talking to a few of us, or a substitute. But other than that, we are there just to learn; we don't bring up subjects about . . . *outside* of school. The only time it comes up if something comes up in school, like a fight or something.

Of course, the relative absence of opportunities to learn in school about contemporary social and cultural issues in the broader community is not the sole reason these teenagers were inexperienced with such research.

Studies show that the television and magazine news media have done a rather poor job of attracting young audiences and educating them about such issues as well. There has been a marked decline over the last two decades of teens and young adults who actually read newsmagazines or watch news on the television (Buckingham, 1997). Even those who are regular viewers of TV news quickly forget most of what they see, and often fail to comprehend it in the first place. As researchers Robinson and Levy conclude:

> Watching the news may produce an experience of having been informed. But it is only a false sense of knowledge, for it is based on a vaguely understood jumble of visual and auditory stimuli that leave few traces in long-term memory. (quoted in Buckingham, 1997, p. 351)

Thus do our institutions of education and journalism teach our youth to be informed and engaged citizens later in life.

## TEACHING AND LEARNING IN THE ZONE OF PROXIMAL DEVELOPMENT

As Dewey has observed, all experiences produce intellectual growth. The question is, in which direction does the growth take place? Some experiences create the conditions for further growth, while others may in fact lead to poor habits that inhibit further occasions for learning (Dewey, 1916). Being dropped into a situation with camera in hand does not in and of itself make for a meaningful learning experience. Even in the most experiential, student-centered classroom, the role of the teacher is essential in shaping, organizing, and directing experiences so the learner can grow and develop through them. To effectively teach students across the field of their experiences, educators must sometimes follow, sometimes lead, and sometimes work with them side by side. No lesson plan can fully map this out. In particular, as in this case at EVC, educators who choose to teach with media must carry in their minds images of potential opportunities, conditions, and levels of learning. The teacher must be ever vigilant, on the lookout for these teachable moments, creating, capturing and exploiting them whenever possible.

It's a complicated dance to do well. On any given day at EVC, there is a complex mix of elements at play that can advance either the sharpening or the dulling of students' capacities for curiosity and wonder. For example, an opportunity to conduct an on-camera interview may for one student be a chance to stretch and grow into a new level of accomplishment. But for another, just seeing and hearing oneself on video may be just one more in a long string of occasions for public failure and humiliation. The teacher must be able to "read" the skill level and learning style of each student and be mindful of what the Russian psycholinguist Vygotsky called the Zone of Proximal Development (ZPD).

According to Vygotsky, this zone is the distance between the actual developmental level as determined by independent problem-solving and the level of potential development as determined through problem-solving under adult guidance or in collaboration with more capable peers. So the teacher arranges for the child to do *with* her what he could not do *without* her. As tutoring proceeds, the child takes over from her parts of the task that he was not able to do at first, but with mastery is consciously able to do under his own control. Vygotsky's theory of learning, as psychologist Jerome Bruner describes it, "presupposes a specific social nature and a process by which children grow into the intellectual life of those around them . . . Thus the notion of a zone of proximal development enables us to propound a new formula, namely that the only good learning is that which is in advance of development" (Bruner, 1986, p. 73).

This theory carries with it the fluid notion of learning where the teacher at times models a task for the students, at other times performs it for the student or performs it alongside the student, and still other times has the student do the task on his own. It is not hard to imagine this in practice with young children where a parent might write on a card, "Happy Birthday, Grandma," for her three-year-old. The child observes her parent write and scribbles a few lines of her own with a crayon. For the next year's birthday greeting, the parent might hold the pen with her four-year-old, guiding the child's hand to form the letters, and then the following year give her a birthday card to look at so the child can copy the words independently.

It is less easy to imagine a teacher going through all these developmental steps for students in, say, the 10th grade. In the day-to-day life of most schools, where the teacher bears the sole and centralized responsibility for teaching, it is nearly impossible for her to devote sufficient attention to any one student in a class of 25, let alone teach to every student's unique and changing zone of proximal development.

In the EVC documentary workshop, the challenges presented by the student/teacher ratio were further complicated by the fact that on any given day each student may be working on a different set of skills. For example, the EVC students were rotated through a range of job responsibilities including camera operation, interviewing, letter writing, logging tapes, and editing, and experienced these various activities as integrated and organic to the production. This is what makes it all so engaging for the student, and so maddeningly difficult for the teacher. The upward arc of student learning (continually refining the same skill) and the lateral arc (broadening their repertoire of skills) were often in motion at the same time.

To teach in such a manner requires a learner-centered methodology. In this kind of classroom the locus of teaching and learning is decentralized. Student work occurs in small groups, individually, and occasionally as a full class. Although the teacher still bears the primary responsibility for mentoring, more often than not he or she makes it happen by creating the conditions for rich student interaction rather than through direct instruction. Engaged in meaningful small-group work, students can act as cognitive amplifiers and reflectors for their peers. In this way, the weight of teaching is distributed. Every student may be called upon at some point to help his or her fellow students to solve a problem, to teach them something he or she is already learning, or to critique their work so they can improve on it next time.

The learner-centered approach carries with it a broad notion that it is the student's questions and concerns that drive the teaching and learning process. Whenever possible, it is the student and not the teacher who does the work of posing and refining questions, finding resources and information, weighing evidence, and crafting a presentation of findings. It also carries the assumption that the boundaries for learning are not limited by the classroom walls. The entire community is a laboratory for learning. Every community member is a potential resource, a potential model and mentor for learning. And every interview experience can provide students with opportunities for further learning.

Visiting such a classroom, one might have the impression that there is no structure or planning determining what the students are learning, for one might see students of diverse skill levels working at a variety of different activities, often independently, without adult supervision. Some might be on the telephone calling to arrange an interview, others might be seated at a video monitor transcribing video footage, and still others might be designing graphics for the opening title sequence. All this without a textbook to guide them in their learning or a final exam to test what they have learned.

Such an impression would be mistaken, since facilitating such a classroom requires a great deal of planning and structure. The teacher needs to work on multiple levels simultaneously, but they all fall within one of two general levels: the process of learning and the process of production. And the teacher needs to make these two processes as public and visible as possible. That is, he or she needs to ensure that the students have a shared sense of the trajectory their project will take—from preproduction, through production, postproduction, and public screening—and the schedule needed to complete each phase. Planning meetings are a feature of the workshop. As much as this is a student-driven project, the fact is that the kids have never made a documentary before. The students need to take ownership of their project and create something they will be proud to show in public. But they can't be expected to move the project through all phases of production unassisted and on schedule. The teacher bears the ultimate responsibility for ensuring that the group meets its deadline and the production results in a finished product.

Throughout the entire production, the teacher also needs to attend to each student's process of learning. From the start, he or she needs to make clear to the students the particular skills they will develop and the methods they will use to assess that development. At EVC, the students are given guidelines and rubrics outlining learning goals in various skill areas that are naturally embedded in the documentary production process, such as research, interviewing, writing, technical arts, editing, and critical viewing. They also are taught to collect samples of their work during the semester in portfolios that provide evidence of their learning in each area. As they edit their own video collections of samples from their first interview and later interviews, or the multiple drafts of narration they wrote, they develop habits of self-reflection and begin to track their own skill development. Engaging students in the assessment of their own work cannot take place only at the end of the semester. It needs to be an organic part of the entire project from start to finish. To truly develop the students' habits of self-reflection, the teacher must develop a portfolio culture in her classroom.

As noted above, at EVC the learner-centered approach for both documentary production and academic skill development is practiced within the context of collaborative group work. This approach presents the teacher with a difficult challenge above and beyond the teaching of cognitive or technical skills. The need to further their emotional and social development is ever present, since the students are put into a situation where they must not only work alongside students from different schools, neighborhoods, and cultural backgrounds, but also forge a common vision of their project. The crew members need to learn to make group decisions throughout the project, including whom they will interview, how the interview will be shot, which footage will get cut, which will be used and in what order, and perhaps most importantly, what music will be used in the opening and closing scenes. So it is critical to the success of this approach for students to learn to listen to all voices in the group and solve problems through group discussions. Learning to come to a collective resolution in a timely manner is also essential, since the group has a deadline by which the tape must be completed and publicly screened. It was the importance of these group social skills that led us to add "Collaborative Group Work" as a distinct portfolio area of skill development.

Over the course of the five-month project, students tend to get passionate about their ideas, and conversations tend to get heated. Group work skills take a lot of time and experience, perhaps a lifetime, to truly master. But once the students successfully work through the challenges of such an experience, they feel great pride in their success. And that feeling stays with them.

In contrast to their traditional teacher-centered classes, students consistently report that they feel more positive about themselves, their work, and their community. A powerful sense of engagement and excitement surrounds them when they are out on the streets talking with their peers, and talking about subjects of immediate importance to them. They have a sense of ownership over their work when they get to decide the subject of study. And they feel tremendous pride when they present their projects and answer questions at public screenings attended by their friends, family, and teachers. As Joseph described it:

> The single most satisfying moment was at the final screening at EVC. I had my mother there, and my girlfriend at the time, and her mother. Her mother didn't know I could speak that well. She had her perceptions about me based on maybe the way I looked or my appearance. She never got a chance to speak with me or find out how I felt. But when she saw me speaking about the project and how proud I was of it, it touched her. . . . seeing my mother in the audience and looking at how proud she was. That sticks out as well.

It is vital for teachers to engage students effectively by developing their sense of empowerment and possibility. This is most commonly understood as student self-expression, or "voice." But this alone is insufficient. Teachers must also grow their students' intellectual capacities by developing their knowledge base and their critical habits of mind. Again, this means teaching to each student's developmental zone, including the particular cultural and linguistic traditions that shape it. So while students may learn to conduct research projects in their own community using only oral anecdotal sources from the streets, they also need to gather written, non-street sources to gain an outsider's perspective. The idea here is to help the students to move beyond themselves and the strictly self-referential to explore other realities; to go outside their own literal, lived experiences to the metaphorical and conceptual realm, and then back again. It means learning to pose their own questions and search for answers to them from multiple perspectives, including the cultural, social, and historical. Teaching these skills might be described as helping students *translate* their own voices into the language of the more formal, dominant culture.

A powerful example of this dual pedagogical approach of community research and translation can be found at the end of the classic ethnographic work *Ways with Words*, in which anthropologist Shirley Brice Heath writes about her experience helping fifth-grade students in the Carolina Piedmont learn to become ethnographers. She relates how she told the students "to imagine they had just been set down as strangers in their own community" (Heath, 1983, p. 317). She directly addresses the gulf that divides the students' familiar, oral community culture and the unfamiliar, written school culture.

> In an effort to have students recognize that spoken and written sources sometimes reinforced and sometimes contradicted each other, the science teacher and I stipulated that answers to each of these questions had to come from at least two sources, one oral and one written. Otherwise the data could not be accepted as reliable. (p. 318)

Through this process, Heath develops the students' abilities to "translate" the social reality of the familiar to the unfamiliar domains. So, for example, she notes that common features of the information gathered from the local community included personalized, contextualized verbal knowledge made up of opinions; narratives with evaluations; and sayings and proverbs. Information in the unfamiliar school domain was depersonalized, decontextualized, and largely written information made up of statements of fact, third-person narratives without evaluation, and written accounts of principles derived from experiments.

In translating from the familiar to the unfamiliar, the students are asked to reflect more deeply on their own taken-for-granted language and culture. They are asked to identify and define the commonsense folk terms and concepts that emerge from their interviews in the community. They are also asked to identify gaps in information between the familiar and unfamiliar domains and formulate specific questions for obtaining the missing information (Heath, 1983, table 9.1, p. 322).

Heath's model of students as translators is unidirectional: from the familiar language of the local community to the unfamiliar language of the school. And in many ways, this is as it should be. She is starting from where the students are and taking them to a new and expanded place beyond that. But in the context of the EVC Documentary Workshop, the students are taking the teacher and the audience who will view their tape from their school language and culture into the students' street culture. The translation goes both ways.

It is of critical importance that the teacher understand this and be willing to truly learn along with and from her students. For the teacher is also a learner who has his or her own particular zone of proximal development, and should always be seeking to learn more beyond that development. Every group of students he or she works with, and every project they embark on together, presents the teacher with a new opportunity to grow.

CHAPTER 3

# *Dreams and Nightmares: A Case Study of Video in a Classroom*

IT WAS ONLY BY THE END of the *Young Gunz* experience, after conducting interviews, shooting footage, and completing editing, that the students involved in the project could begin to understand how all the various parts of their project fit together. It was only after they presented their tape to the public that they could really understand the kind of impact their own creation had on an audience. Yet, as intensive a learning experience as the project was for them, the 18 weeks they had to work on *Young Gunz* was simply not sufficient time to close their literacy gaps, which had taken over 16 years of formal and informal education to develop. Making one documentary about gun violence could not give the students the experience that would be necessary for such a broad and lasting impact. There were too many new layers of skills and habits for the students to absorb in too short a time. They had only just taken the first steps in learning to ask their own questions and to speak through the language of images. To really have exercised and grown their skills, the students would have needed a repeat of the workshop experience; the community-based video experience would have to have been a part of their regular school curriculum as well as their after-school experiences. We don't expect children to learn to write well from just one essay or poetry project. Literacy skills develop over years of repeated practice in countless different situations. The same holds true for learning to produce community media projects: the skills take time and practice to develop.

Imagine for a moment what it would be like if schools—from the elementary level through senior high—routinely offered kids the opportunity to conduct in-depth explorations of subjects that drew upon a range of disciplines, including science, history, and language arts. Furthermore if schools also provided students with a broad range of media tools—video, photography, film, print magazine, radio, webzine, or multimedia—with which to conduct their inquiries and present their work to a community audience, the students' repertoire of critical literacy skills would be that much more deepened and refined with each new project experience.

That is, as long as the approach to teaching with and about the media takes a holistic view of the learner. A student's intellectual growth is deeply tangled up with his or her emotional and psychological development. This is particularly the case with adolescents whose families and community support systems have been damaged for a very long time. While they may try to hide it from peers and adults, these teens bring their fragile state of mental health to school with them every day. Teachers who know their students well will notice how the alienation and hopelessness these students suffer from overwhelms their capacity for curiosity and study. They are too preoccupied and distracted to focus on the tasks at hand. So teaching media in the classroom, or any subject for that matter, must address students' cognitive and affective capacities. To separate the two would risk perpetuating the underdevelopment of their minds and spirits.

In this scenario, rigor would be married to the relevance of personal and community inquiries. Developing literacy and critical thinking skills would be embedded in the exploration of those issues that cause so many students to become alienated and withdraw from learning in the first place. School projects would give space for inquiries into personal and family subjects such as teen depression, eating disorders, and domestic violence. The disconnect between the students' in-school and out-of-school experiences could be bridged, and the intellectual gaps could be significantly narrowed.

Rethinking school along these lines has been at the heart of EVC's education reform and professional development work since the mid-1980s. While the Doc Workshop and EVC's other programs take place outside of the conventional school setting, EVC has used a capacity-building strategy—including professional development and ongoing classroom support for teachers—to integrate its model of community video inquiry into the everyday curricula of school. The degree to which it is possible to adapt the methodology of the EVC community video workshop, as described in the previous chapter, into a classroom setting is a measure of its institutional scalability. That is to say, the more we understand about how a media-based pedagogy fits into the life of a class, the more possible it will be to make a large-scale change in the way teaching and learning are practiced.

What, then, does it look like when students in the classroom practice this kind of community-based and learner-centered media work? What kind of learning takes place when EVC's after-school documentary workshop model is implemented in a classroom setting? Which practices change, and which ones remain the same? And how do the students experience the lesson?

In an attempt to address these questions, I conducted a case study of a video documentary class in a school I will call East City High School, visiting the students in the class on a weekly basis as they worked on their project over the course of a semester. In the main project the class took on, a hidden but all-too-pervasive problem was explored: depression and suicide among students at East City High. The teacher, whom I will call Christina, was in her second year of teaching in the public schools. Prior to her job at East City, for 20 years she had been a professional sculptor and painter. During her first year at the school, she attended an EVC professional development workshop. There she met EVC's media education teacher consultant, whom I will call Marie, who asked her whether she wanted assistance in leading a documentary video class at her school. Christina said she did want to conduct a video workshop with her students, and Marie agreed to provide her with assistance in planning and facilitating the class on a weekly basis.

From Christina's perspective, this was an opportunity to engage her students in a new way of learning: getting them out into the community and allowing them to use media for both self-expression and research into the issues that are of most concern to them. From Marie's perspective, it was an opportunity to integrate the EVC model into the life of the school, and to help develop Christina's skills so that she would later be able to facilitate an engaging and rigorous community project with video on her own.

This chapter sketches out Christina's and Marie's experiences in incorporating the Doc Workshop into the classroom. After providing some background information to set the context, I will let the voices of the students and descriptions of the images from their video tell the story of the documentary class and the way it fit into their larger community experiences.

## SETTING THE CONTEXT: A COMMUNITY UNDER SIEGE

East City High School is a small alternative high school located in a New York City district with a strong history of progressive school reform. With 320 students and 24 staff members and teachers, it occupies one floor of a building that also houses three other schools. It opened in the early 1990s, part of a heady period of growth and optimism for the small schools movement. But it was also a time of violence and despair for the community it was established to serve. Through the 1980s and 1990s, this community—predominantly poor and working-class Puerto Rican and African American families—was ravaged by the twin epidemics of AIDS and crack cocaine. A people full of hope and promise watched as their neighbors, friends, and family members wasted away. They struggled to survive as drug wars exploded on the streets around them.

By the start of the new millennium, the fury of these plagues and wars had largely been spent. No one can say exactly how or why it happened. Perhaps crack simply fell out of fashion, replaced by Ecstasy and other more psychedelic drugs. The police certainly played a big role, as regular invasions of SWAT teams who fancied themselves as cowboy commandos swept the streets clean of swaggering kids in gravity-defying baggy pants who fancied themselves as outlaw gangsters. The male population of whole neighborhoods seemed to be forcibly relocated into prisons, turning construction and management of prisons into a booming industry. The full count of the dead and wounded is recorded only in the memories of the survivors and in the memorials painted on building walls.

How does one take measure of the human wreckage? The number of babies born addicted to crack? Or born infected with HIV? The number of listless men and women in line outside the shopping centers waiting to cash in their day's hunt of bottles and cans? Or the number of kids growing up in jail?

In a broad sense, it could be said that East City High School (along with most other New York City alternative schools) was established to help kids build their intellectual, social, and emotional capacities so they could work their way out of the zone where these questions become necessary. But effectively teaching academic subjects to troubled students requires a powerful and wide-ranging repertoire that few teachers possess.

Recruiting and retaining teachers who can truly cultivate students' intellectual, social, and emotional capacities, the so-called habits of mind and habits of heart, is of course a colossal challenge for any school. At East City, this is especially apparent in the school's personnel profile: turnover at East City is a yearly ritual. Approximately 60 percent of the teachers have been teaching there for three years or less. And approximately 60 percent have been teaching anywhere for three years or less. Only two teachers remain from the original staff of seven years ago. The founding principal resigned in 2001. Four teachers left around the same time.

## THE CLASS

I visited East City High periodically during the year Christina taught the video documentary class. For me, the class presented an opportunity to explore a number of questions, both theoretical and practical, that have preoccupied me over the years. My overarching interest was in better understanding the kinds of literacies that are developed and the kind of learning that takes place when EVC's model of community-based media education is practiced in a school setting. I wanted to find out, for example, what capacities are demanded of the classroom teacher and student? What kind of teaching and learning does the model make possible that otherwise wouldn't take place? How and to what extent does it develop the students' critical thinking and language skills—spoken, visual and written—and what role does the social context of the documentary class and the surrounding community play in such development? What problems, tensions, and challenges does this kind of teaching and learning create, particularly in a school setting?

As for my role in the class, I was a researcher, and although I tried to observe as much as possible, I was not always detached or silent in my role. It was my informal agreement with the teacher and students that if I was going to be observing and interviewing the students, often with a video camera, the least I could do would be to lend a helping hand. There were times when I added a comment, posed a question in the group discussion, or helped one group of students set up a camera while the teacher was busy with others. There were also times when I brought in an article or resource that I thought might be useful or stayed after class to give the teacher suggestions regarding the pace or structure of the class.

The class's story, like that of any class, is a narrative with multiple layers and perspectives. Meeting on alternate days for an hour and a half per session, the students in the class—eight female and eight male—were mostly 10th and 11th graders who had had little, if any, prior video experience. They were a mixed group in terms of their academic skill level.

Their story is linear, following the structured stages of video production. But there is a nonlinear aspect to the tale, consisting of the learning process that constantly interrupts the description of how the students created their video. Many small individual and group experiences happened along the way, some the predictable product of developmental lessons, some the spontaneous eruption of circumstance. The students' story, as much as it is about the production of a video and the development of a learning process, also turns out to be about a web of relationships: those that formed between learner and learner, learner and teacher, learner and documentarian, learner and subject matter, and learner and video technology.

To capture some of this multiplicity, I will examine the question at hand through three different lenses: the pedagogical, the theoretical, and the visual. Pedagogical questions naturally surface as specific strategies for teaching and learning. I raise some theoretical concerns related to broader questions of learning, literacy, and culture. I make a special effort to give the reader more of the raw visual and aural data generated by the class, and some of my personal responses to them, so that a fuller, more textured sense of the people and the conversations can emerge.

I include transcripts of verbal classroom talk along with descriptions of the visual body language that accompanied it, all excerpted from videotapes that either I or the students have shot. While my aim is for authenticity, the reader must remember that regardless of how authentic the language sounds or looks, it has for the most part arrived on the printed page after first being framed, filtered, and recorded through a video camera, with the viewfinder pressed to my eye or the students'.

What follows, then, are conversations and learning experiences that are clustered roughly around the four following documentary-based activities: logging, choosing a topic, interviewing, and reflections. They are singular in that they are rooted in a particular time and place. But they are also transcendent in that they speak to broader questions and concerns and have, for me, revealed deeper truths.

## LOGGING

*Miss, don't keep stopping the tape every three seconds.*—Jackson

Logging is the tedious but indispensable process of writing down all of the dialogue, sounds, and camera shots recorded on a videotape, along with judgments as to their quality and possible use in a final video. Creating a written record of what is on a video is an essential step in the process of making a documentary. This record is used as a guide for a video editor to know first what material she has to work with, and second, where in the hours and hours of footage on the tape she can locate each word and image that make up the material she wants. After the logging process is completed, editors use the written logs to compose an edit plan or edit decision list (also known as an EDL).

Logging requires students to attend closely to the sights and sounds on the screen, in all their detail. Through the process, students develop observation skills. They become intimately familiar with all aspects of the footage available for a given project, learning to separate out sound from picture, and learning to imagine how the disparate pieces might be pulled from their original context and reordered in a future edit of the tape. For example, the annoying noise of a siren from a police car driving by, which may have interrupted a street interview, might be used with other images to create a sense of urban chaos and danger in a completely different scene.

Logging helps students exercise their imagination when considering what a final product might look like once the parts of the tape are rearranged. The judgments they note in the log are ultimately used to inform decisions about what stays in and what gets cut. The entire logging process feeds the imagination with raw material that can then be molded into something greater than the sum of its parts.

**Learning to Log**

Christina's class meets in the science lab, the only room available at that period of the day. Students sit on metal stools around the high fixed workstations, which hold sinks with shiny gas nozzles and protruding metal rods. This is not the most conducive environment for discussions—students can't face each other seated in circles or even semicircles. But it will have to do.

Today the class gathers around a cart that holds a VCR and a video monitor. Christina inserts a VHS cassette and presses the "PLAY" button. A conversation from the streets outside the classroom window comes to life on the screen:

"Hello. I'm Jackson from East City High and we're interviewing . . ."

The boy speaking stands tall in his black leather jacket and black wool cap covering a black do-rag, more than a head taller than the woman standing next to him. He points the microphone to the woman and she answers, "Wanda Smith."

They stand with their backs against a storefront window that reflects cars passing by and the fire escape on the building across the street.

"Well, really we interviewing people just about dreams." Pausing, he quickly glances down at his paper with interview questions on it. "Have you achieved your dreams?"

She pauses, sighs, and says, "No. Not quite."

"Well, what was your dream?"

The woman stands facing the camera but looking sideways at Jackson. "Umm." She swallows and continues. "Well, growing up I wanted to be a pediatrician."

Another student holding a microphone questions another person on the street.

"Have you achieved your dreams?" The student interviewer has her hair in braids. She speaks to a woman with gold hoop earrings. It is a medium shot. The student and the woman are in shadow in the foreground. Behind them the intersection is full of movement and action. "No, I didn't."

"What was your dream?"

"To finish high school. But I had a baby, and then I got my GED. But I was twenty-eight when I got it. I was hoping to go back, to go back to school. It's just that now I got a one-year-old. Now I have to look for a baby-sitter."

After several more video segments that show other student interviewers stopping individuals on the street, the tape stops and Christina turns off the video monitor. There is a buzz in the room. The students are excited about the responses they got from the people they interviewed when they went out in the neighborhood the week before. They were working on their class "practice project": East City Dreams. They had expected no one would want to talk with them, but instead, people had lined up to be interviewed. Some people had even asked them if they were from Nickelodeon.

Marie explains to the students that they will need to log the tapes they shot and hands out a log sheet containing three columns: the Tape Time, the Name or Description of Interviewee, and the Summary of Interviewee's Points. She plays a tape to go over the method of logging for everyone. After a moment, she stops the tape and asks, "What did she say? Was this important?" One student, Jackson, complains, "Miss, don't keep stopping the tape every three seconds."

Christina notes, "It is laborious to do, but you have to do it. Summarize what you think is important. You have to write down every point they make except that if it is off the topic. So let's divide into our groups."

The students divide into four teams, each assigned to log the tape they shot. Talk and laughter fill the room. Jackson complains again, "Why can't we just keep letting the tape go and write it after?" Christina comes by Jackson's group and asks if they are working together and stopping the tape.

"Yo, Jonathan! You see the Lexus?" asks Jackson. He is excited by the car he notices passing by in their video.

On the monitor, Jackson's voice can be heard saying, "Uh . . . this is Jackson . . . Peace." They watch that section three or four times, laughing each time. Jackson, the interviewer, had been caught off guard. He couldn't think of what else to ask the interviewee, and so the interview ended abruptly. He had a surprised look on his face.

The three students watching the tape rarely stop it to write anything. They laugh at the way some of the people interviewed looks (a man who is missing teeth) and talk about camera work that was shaky or not well framed. ("It is curved . . . Look at how it is slanted.")

Logging requires students to perform a complex set of skills: attend simultaneously to both the visual and spoken information flowing from the screen; summarize in written form what is seen and heard; and make judgments about the material's potential value for a final tape. To accomplish each of these tasks, students need to be able to move across modes of literacy from the concrete to a more abstract plane where they can make broader connections to things not on the screen—where they can look for patterns and pose more questions.

They also need to bring a critical distance to the material they are viewing. Naming and discussing the problems the people on the streets spoke about meant, in some instances, raising issues that they themselves faced in their own families. For the students in Christina's class, the closeness and relevance of the content were both engaging and distancing, something that they wanted to talk about but also wanted to avoid.

Finally, there was the issue of not wanting to stop the tape and write down what was seen. One reason why this was difficult for the students was that it required them to make decisions about the relative value of the data they were gathering before they ever had the experience of editing their tape. To make judgments about which images and statements should be used and which should be left out, the students needed to already carry with them a fairly developed picture of what the final tape would look and sound like. Few of the students had such a picture in their minds in order to determine whether a newly taped bit of material could fit or not.

The resistance to stopping the tape, I believe, speaks to a deeper contradiction when the expected habits of school behavior come into conflict with the expected habits of media viewing out of school. Although they are clearly not the same thing, most students, and people in general, have the expectation that they should engage and interact with video the same way they do with TV, so they approach the act of watching video in school much in the same way they watch television outside of school. From this perspective, it is understandable that watching themselves on video provoked the "Hey, look, that's me on TV!" kind of excitement that it did. In general, the students were drawn to the look of things—how they, their classmates, and the people they interviewed looked on camera. And there was interest in, and recognition of, the "bloopers" genre of material, too, the humorous mistakes captured on camera.

Logging the video footage places the students in the familiar position of watching television. It would be painfully disruptive to turn off the television every half-minute or so, and as Jackson pointed out, it is intolerable to stop the videotape what felt like to him "every three seconds." Of course, television is full of interruptions, jumps, breaks, and non sequiturs, but it is still all accepted as part of an uninterrupted flow.

Bringing video into the classroom places in-school and out-of-school media viewing habits in tension with each other. It is also useful to place this kind of teaching to attend to detail in the broader cultural context of a media-saturated society that, as art historian Jonathan Crary describes, is in "an ongoing crisis of inattentiveness." He argues that the sensory overload of our high-tech society is a historical and economic development to the point where our lives have become a patchwork of disconnected states. The positive spin for this state of being is called multitasking. The capacity for "paying attention" is also a capacity for living with distraction as our culture "continually push(es) attention and distraction to new limits and thresholds, with an endless sequence of new products, sources of stimulation, and streams of information, and then respond with new methods of managing and regulating perception" (Crary, 1999, pp. 13–14).

Teaching students to look closely over and over again until the elements of a given scene can be pulled apart—the words, rhythms of speech, hand gestures, movement of the eyes, tilt of the head, style of dress, color of skin, and activity in the background—only to reconnect them again with new meaning requires sustained and critical attention that is different from, in fact counter to, this historical cultural trend. But students can and do learn how to attend to such details, and to make connections and meaning from them. With practice, they can learn to slow down and read video footage as the text that it is. In the case of the East City students, after much struggle they eventually did log their footage and edit their "Dreams" tape.

## CHOOSING A GROUP TOPIC

*We are dealing with things outside the school. We're finding out what is going on with other people's lives. How the society runs and how people feel about what is going on here and there*—Jackson

Engaging students in the study of youth-related and community-based issues of their own choosing is not a novel idea. A small but vocal group of educators has promoted this sort of approach to learning at least since the 1960s. And some of those efforts trace their inspiration back to John Dewey and the progressive movements of the earlier part of the 20th century. Projects that strongly emphasize experiential learning—such as Expeditionary Learning Outward Bound, the internship model of the City-As-School network, and the service learning movement in general—all practice this kind of youth engagement. This same approach is the foundation of Foxfire's educational philosophy (Wigginton, 1986), the science inquiry method of the Lillian Weber's Workshop Center (Weber and Alberty, 1997), and has become a teaching strategy commonly used in the National Writing Project literacy repertoire. In each case, it has been argued that the learner learns best when she can personally connect to and engage with the subject matter at hand.

## Learning to Choose a Group Topic

Following in this tradition, Christina assumed a few givens that determined the structure of her video class; these were adopted from the EVC model. First, the students would investigate a social problem or question of direct relevance to their lives. Second, they would decide as a group what the subject of their inquiry would be. Third, they would collectively produce a documentary about it. Last, they would focus on a skill area and collect evidence of their growth in that area.

The process of exercising student choice is just that: a process. In this class, the students were guided through an intense experience of looking inward and outward, revealing painful personal stories, viewing other student documentaries, probing ideas, and gathering peer support for their ideas. It took three days of class for the students to agree on a common subject for their video project.

The class had just completed their three-week *Dreams* project, which was designed to briefly take them through the steps of shooting and editing a video. Now they were starting their major project for the rest of the semester, and the first thing they needed to do was choose a question or problem to explore.

There is a buzz in the class that continues despite Christina's efforts to quiet everyone down. She tries again.

"Okay, guys, we need to get serious here. What are we gonna do next?"

"I was thinking about that subject that we were talking about before. Youth in prisons," offers one student.

"Youth in prisons!" Christina repeats loudly. She goes to the board and writes it down. "Why?"

"Because it is a subject that all of us deal with every day. None of us can say that we don't have friends that are in jail." Nervous laughter erupts from her classmates.

"Okay, Majandra thinks it is an important theme because it impacts all of us. Okay, what else?"

A girl wearing a gauzy veil of a scarf over her braided hair picks her head up off the desk where she was resting and says, "Police brutality and racism."

A voice from further back in the room can be heard. It's Julius, a tall, stocky African American boy with closely shaved hair. "I think we should do peer pressure. The pressure on youth going into prison."

Christina pushes him further. "This is really important. I really want you to think about concrete things. Like Julius, if you were to do peer pressure. What would you do? Who would you interview?"

He pauses and slowly responds with just one word, "Gangs."

Remembering she wanted them to do more than just talk about it, Christina switches gears and asks, "Did you write about it? Pull out your journals. I want to hear what you wrote. Who has something that they can read? This was a big part of your journal entry. You needed to defend your topic. What don't you know about it? What do you want to find out?"

The energy generated by talk a few moments earlier is gone. At the mention of writing, the classroom goes flat, like a tire that just had the air let out from it. Kids open their notebooks and leaf through the pages; maybe they are just going though the motions. No one comes up with anything they might have written. Time runs out.

The next time the class meets, Christina picks up where she left off. She is pushing and prodding the students to do something they are stubbornly resisting: write about an issue or problem they want to investigate for their tape.

Gail's broad face turns to Christina. Her big, round eyes close tight for a moment. She can't seem to hold back any longer. "Listen!"

"I *am* listening. I know you don't know what to write. But you have to try."

"I don't know what topic to choose. I really don't!"

"So choose two."

"I don't want to choose none!" Gail turns away now.

Christina looks a bit frustrated and baffled by the resistance she is encountering. After all, in the tradition of student-centeredness, she is giving the students the freedom to choose their own topic. They should be animated and engaged.

Perhaps the students aren't used to having this kind of freedom. They aren't comfortable with it, don't know what to do with it, and so they give it back to the teacher. And perhaps Gail's resistance is rooted in the fact that she is being asked to do something that she never learned to do before: use writing to explore and develop her ideas. And not only that: she is being asked to use writing to dig deep and come up with an idea that will have great significance. It is not just some idle assignment that will be handed in to the teacher, read and graded only by her, and never looked at again. This is an idea that will be presented to and considered by the whole class. It's an idea that might guide the class for the rest of the semester. This is a high-stakes idea. There is a lot of responsibility attached to the freedom Christina is pushing onto the students.

Christina hands out papers to the students. She wants them to brainstorm project ideas and the questions that they have about each one.

"Okay, let's write down the list of subjects we have discussed. And if you have any new ones you'd like to put on the plate. Youth in jail was one. Up at the board."

Jackson is wearing a two-colored baseball cap today, half blue, half orange, turned backward over a black do-rag. He raises his hand, "Miss, could I ask you a question right quick? Could I ask you a question right quick?"

"What?"

"It doesn't make sense, like the way you say, like pick, like pick a topic and then, and then ask yourself about. You said, 'What you wanna learn more about it.' But . . . we pick a topic that we really know about. And really wanna do about. So we can't really talk about, like . . ." He is searching for the right words to explain his confusion.

"You already know everything about it?" Christina offers.

"That's what I'm saying." Jackson affirms.

Jackson was describing what seemed to be a paradox. The class was being asked to look at a problem that they already see around them in their daily lives. He raised a key problem for the teacher: How to guide the learner from the known to the unknown, through Vygotsky's famous zone of proximal development. As science educator Mark St. John explained it,

> In the bubble of the known, you are surrounded by a model of the world that explains things to you, and fits with what you know. In that sphere it all makes sense. Then you discover the boundaries and limitations of your model. . . . And for a child, you are always looking for that door from the known to the unknown, where you can press forth and push, and in a sense expand the bubble of the known. But it has to be proximal. If it is too far away, it is not useful. (St. John, 1999, p. 13)

The entire documentary-making process seemed to be about pushing through the door from the known to the unknown. The teacher's job was to make sure the learner was continually expanding the bubble.

Gail says what she seems to have wanted to say all along: "Why don't *you* make up a topic!"

The back and forth continues. The students watch to see if the teacher will back down. She doesn't. Instead, she repeats her intention once more: "I want you guys to figure out what *you* want to do."

Later she adds: "You can dream up anything you want. You can do any subject you want. If you can think of a plan of how to do it . . . I want you to want to do what we do. Otherwise it is going to be boring."

The students sit quietly, looking down at floor. Monica has her baseball cap over her face. Gail looks sullen. Crystal breaks the silence, saying tentatively: "We could do a skit."

"Let's do . . . Oh, I got it!" Jackson suddenly gets up, goes to the board, and writes: Why do people think about suicide?

"I think that is a very good topic," says Majandra with a nod of approval.

"I don't want to do that," says Crystal, shaking her head and swiveling in her chair. She is visibly uncomfortable.

"There's people out here who have personal experience," says Majandra quietly.

"Some people think life is hard," says Jackson, defending his idea. "Some people think they shouldn't be here. Some people just ain't got nothing up here," he says, pointing to his head.

"Okay, everybody take ten minutes," Christina says. "I want you all to write. Answer the six questions. Then we will talk about it."

Time passes while the students write, heads bent over their desks. They address questions designed to help them develop their topic ideas into a treatment for their video project, such as: What is your essential question? Why do you want to make a video about this question? What other things do you want to find out about it? What people would you like to interview to learn more about it? What images or scenes would you like to shoot to make a tape about that topic? Who is the intended audience for your tape?

Finally, Christina breaks the silence. She asks for volunteers to read what they've written.

A soft-spoken voice can be heard from the side of the classroom: "I wrote about unprotected sex, teen pregnancy, and why some teens neglect their child."

"Okay, so let's hear what you wrote."

"All right." He looks down at his paper. His hair is braided in cornrows. A light mustache and even lighter beard provide scant cover on his soft but acne-scarred face.

> I would like to produce this topic because today many teens are having babies and some teens, mostly males, do not care for their

child. This is important because every child needs a mother and father. I would like to know why teens have unprotected sex. And when they know what could happen but they do not take responsibility. Children should not be denied love and care. Every child wants someone to love them. Especially their parents. Teens having babies also leads to dropping out of school.

Majandra reads next:

The two topics that we brainstormed about were youth in jail and why people think about suicide. Youth in jail and peer pressure tie in together and it is a topic that most teens are involved in today. We could find statistics about how many youth are in jail and how many of them are in gangs. We could learn about what goes on in Riker's Island by interviewing one or two inmates. We could also interview someone who is there.

The suicide topic is good because it is surprising how many people have tried it and done it who are around my age. We could interview those who have tried it, a parent or a friend of a person who has done it, and we will find out how it affects them. I am sorry to say that I could be interviewed.

Okay, now interviews. People for the youth in prison: you could interview somebody who is there, a gang member, a corrections officer—if they are allowed to do it—or a lawyer.

For the other one, it's a tryer, a family member, a psychologist, and somebody who has been in an institution for that reason.

Our primary audience would be young urban youths who are part of these problems. Questions we could ask them are: How does peer pressure affect you? How many youths are in jail? How many jailed youths are in gangs? What is life like in Rikers?

Suicide: How many youths have tried it? How many have succeeded? Why do these youths do it? And what is treatment like for these youths? Is it good, is it bad and what do they do for you?

Majandra finishes reading and looks up from her notebook.

The bell rings and the students get up to leave. Christina tells them to prepare to continue the discussion on the next class day. That day comes, and Christina jumps right back into the question at hand:

"Last week there were about four people who read their treatments on what the subject was that they wanted to do. We are going to finish reading everybody's and then we are going to vote. We are going to decide what our topic is going to be. . . . Who else has not read? . . . Monica. Do you want to talk about a subject, even though you didn't write?"

Sitting off to the side of the room, Monica looks to be a study in black and red: Her long black hair falls down over her black shirt. Black eyeliner accentuates her large eyes. The shiny red lollipop she is sucking on matches the shiny red lipstick she has on. She begins to speak slowly.

"Okay. I wanted to write about suicide and depression. But since that day, I got really, really, like, angry. And I didn't want to say anything cause I figured . . . and then somebody else suggested it and then . . . 'Cause we should find out what causes that . . ."

Jackson interjects with a one-word answer, "Stress."

Monica continues, ". . . what goes, through people's minds, especially teenagers . . ."

He interrupts again, "It's all in people's minds, in people's minds . . ."

"I'm not finished yet!" shouts Monica.

"Take your time, take your time. Jackson! Let Monica finish. Don't interrupt! Let her finish."

"I can't do this."

"Keep talking," Christina coaches her. "Can you do it without the sucker, Monica?"

"Well, nobody's listening to me, so . . ." her voice trails off as she takes the lollipop out of her mouth.

"Just hold it when you talk." This provokes much laughter and some bawdy comments by some of the boys.

"All right . . ." Monica takes a breath and starts again. "'Cause I know a lot of teenagers that have attempted suicide and failed." She picks at her eyebrow as she ponders what she will say next. "I'm not gonna say any names." A nervous, toothy smile slowly comes across face. "I happen to be one myself. Okay, I'm not gonna die." She waves her hand as if to hold off an expected flood of pity and concern. "I was locked up in the hospital for two weeks for that."

"Damn!" A voice of shock and amazement comes from the back of the room. It sounds like Julius.

"They had me on medication." Her hand is now slowly combing its way through her hair.

"We didn't ask you about that. About that subject. I'm serious," grumbles Jackson. He is visibly disturbed. Maybe he knew this was coming and was intentionally trying to shut down her story.

Monica leans forward, and yells, "Nobody asked you if you asked me!"

Jackson shakes his head and looks down at the floor. "That's not right, man. We talking about the subject, not what happened to y'all . . ."

Julius adjusts his blue Cleveland Indians baseball cap and raises his hand. "Why, why were you so mad? Why, why, why'd you want to, um . . ." He searches for the right words. ". . . take that attempt?"

"'Cause life sucked." Monica holds her lollipop in her right hand and grabs onto the metal rod rising out of the science lab table with her left. "That was basically my reason. 'Cause I had a lot of family problems and stuff. That was the problem. I had a lot of family problems. I had a lot of social issues. People who were around . . . You know, life wasn't going well for me. I wanted to end it, yeah." She sticks the lollipop back in her mouth but still holds onto the rod.

Julius continues with his line of inquiry. "What make you fail your attempt?"

"Um . . . it didn't work. I tried taking a whole bunch of aspirins. It just made me feel high. It didn't kill me. And then, I threatened to kill myself. And then, my grandmother called the cops and they went and took me away to the hospital. They had me in there. It was horrible."

Melika asks, "You had to share a room with a crazy person? Huh?"

"You weren't crazy. You just had to go through some problems," says Julius.

"Yeah. They were crazy 'cause they attempted to do it. I attempted, too. But they had. . ." She illustrates what she means by running an imaginary razor up and down the veins of her wrist. ". . . marks. I haven't gone to that extreme. I cut myself. Yeah." She turns her wrist over now and makes a cutting movement on the back of her hand. Suddenly interested in her hands, she inspects them in more detail. "I have scars. But . . ." Her voice trails off.

"Majandra's also said she'd be willing to talk about it, as well," says Christina.

"You tried to kill yourself?"

"Yeah, all right. Here it goes." She pushes back her hair, but it falls back over her long, oval face. She leaves it that way. She is wearing a loose-fitting black t-shirt.

"Um, I got a lot of problems at home. A lot of problems at home. Between me and my parents, family things, social things. A lot of stuff." Her nasal voice, sounding like she has a bad cold, gets louder and faster. "You know, I just finished having an argument with my parents in the other house. And it wasn't the first time that I did this, when I did it again. See, like, I went home. I was crying. And I don't like being in the house alone. 'Cause I start thinking depressing, I start thinking about crap . . ." She raises both hands to her head, index finger pointed to each temple, with her other fingers spread out below. "I, I was just mad. And I was talking to one of my cousins on the phone and I was telling him how I felt."

Now she is really picking up speed.

> They were like, "Yo, but don't worry about it. Things'll get better. Things'll get better." And I was like, "No they're not." I told him I was gonna do it and he said, "No, don't do that." But then he had to hang up the phone with me. So, whatever. Then I called one of my other friends and I told her I was gonna do it. I put in on her voice mail and then I hung up. So I was looking around the house for something to do it with. And I found a bottle of Dimetapp. Believe it or not, it would have worked. I don't sound like it would've but it would've. It was a bottle of grape Dimetapp. And I read it and it said, *Keep out of reach of children*. So I grabbed it. Took it. And then my cousin called me and she was like, "Yo! Come on! Why'd you do that? What's wrong with you?" And started crying and everything. She came to my house and dragged me out the house and took me to the hospital. My parents didn't know that I did it. I had to stay in the hospital like, a good thirteen hours. I had a guard watching me, they took they took all my clothes 'cause they thought I was gonna try it again. I had to talk to a bunch of psychiatrists. I was this close to going into the facility but they wouldn't take me. Because I begged them not to go. I have to go to counseling at least twice a week every week now.

Christina moves the discussion on to another student. "What about you, Gail?"

"You wanted to do suicide, too?" Julius asks, perhaps bracing himself for another sad story.

"I have a lot of friends that are in the hospital right now," says Gail.

"Damn! Life must suck for ya'll," responds Julius. Gail laughs at this.

"No I'm serious," Julius says, shaking his head. "That ain't no joke. Damn . . ." Clearly bothered by it all, he later adds:

> I don't even think that teenagers should be thinking about stuff like that. Stuff like that, your mind shouldn't be taking your life . . . When you're sixteen you s'pposed to be thinking about school, you s'pposed to be thinking about getting new friends, you s'pposed to be thinking about stuff like that. You aint s'pposed to be thinking about killing yourself. I'm not mad at y'all but, you gotta shake that stuff off, daddy! You only live once.

Majandra tries to help him understand how it was. "'Cause when life gets messed up, like you start thinking about how can you fix the messed-up thing. And if you feel it's never gonna stop getting messed up, the, the only thing you can think about of ending it all being messed is ending it all completely."

"You kill yourself you just make it worse for your family," Julius responds.

"Most people, why you think about killing yourself? It's *because* of your family," says Gail.

"It is hard to understand, Julius." Christina's tone is soft and sympathetic. "If you never experienced it, it's hard to understand. It really is."

"To be that depressed, it's hard for someone who is not depressed to really understand that," adds Marie.

"When you going through all that stuff, and there's nobody there to talk to at that moment, you don't *think* that anybody *cares,*" Majandra says with great emphasis on the words "think" and "cares." "I didn't notice that anybody cared until *after* it happened. And when I hit that hospital and there were ten people in my room and there were only supposed to be two."

Christina uses this last comment to bring some closure to the discussion. "So one thing that we could do if we did this video would be to, to somehow figure out how to help people who are feeling this way. So that they know that people care about them in their life. It seems like we have a lot to say on this issue."

"We should do this issue," says Majandra.

"We should do this issue," echoes Gail.

"This is definitely the most interesting discussion we have had. You guys have a lot to say on this subject . . . Okay, so let's go ahead and vote." Christina counts the hands raised for each of six possible documentary topics that have emerged over the days of discussion.

Suicide wins by a landslide. The class chooses to produce a video documentary that would try to answer the question first posed a week earlier by Jackson: Why do people think about committing suicide?

Perhaps it was the courage that Monica and Majandra summoned up that was the determining factor in the students' decision, their willingness to tell those dark and terrible stories, to let loose their private pain in the public space of school, and damn the consequences. Or maybe it was the sheer excitement and drama of it all. Maybe it was the sense that the rest of the class had of being let in on secrets that have no business being talked about in school, no legitimate place within the academic curriculum, that engaged and persuaded everyone, secrets of the deepest, most frightening kind. Clearly, this daytime TV talk show–style of confessional conversation was outside the predictable, textbook-driven "How many pages does it have to be?" and "Will it be in the test?" kind of discourse that usually governs classroom discussion.

Whatever the reason, the class had successfully concluded the first stage of their documentary inquiry. They had brainstormed, written, and publicly presented their ideas, questioned each other, argued, told stories, listened, struggled with what they were hearing, and arrived at the other end of it all collectively exercising student choice in determining their research subject.

Along the way, the students overcame their initial reluctance and took their first steps to use writing as a means of working out their ideas. They also grew more comfortable with the notion that their ideas count, will be respected and considered, and might well determine the course of study for the rest of the class.

This process was a demanding one for students and teacher. It required that the students take real risks with their ideas and questions. This would have been true even if the subject matter had not been so deeply personal, but was all the more so in this case. It required the teacher to build a safe and trusting environment that could support such risk-taking. As every teacher knows, maintaining such a learning environment over the course of a semester can be a Sisyphean task, since classes are made up of a fragile web of relationships that need to be woven, patched up, and rewoven with almost every new encounter.

In the very next class, the boulder of group decision-making had to be rolled back up the mountain again. Jonathan, a student who had been absent for the last few days, made his presence well known when he vehemently objected to the topic that had been chosen. The tearing and patching up of this part of the class web presents rich opportunities for learning about group dynamics and the complicated role I played as documenter with a camera.

The students are watching a documentary produced by students at EVC exploring the pros and cons of marijuana legalization. It is an introductory media literacy lesson designed to get the students familiar with the basic elements of the documentary genre: the interviews, archival footage, narration, music, and so on. As the images fly by, Christina shouts out, "Remember, watch the different elements. The style, the effects. Keep mental notes."

Afterward, Marie passes out sheets with questions about the tape. Some students are answering the questions; others are organizing their notebooks into specific sections for this project. Jonathan discovers what the subject of the class project is and loudly complains, "This is a topic for somebody who should be locked up in a mentally insane hospital."

Christina is at his desk trying to soften his rising hostility. "This will prevent people—this is a topic to help people who feel this way. So maybe we could help them not to feel that way."

"I don't see nobody in here that wanna kill theyself."

"Well, you missed the whole conversation. We had several people in here who have felt that way."

"Who? Who?"

"You should have been here." Christina appears to be withholding the identities of those students who spoke publicly during the last class, protecting them from the anger, frustration, and perhaps fear he is voicing. Not having been part of that emotionally bonding experience, he is an outsider who needs to be brought into the group.

"Who? Tell me," he insists.

Jonathan puts his head down on the tabletop. His hair is tightly braided in cornrows coming down in short tails in the back. The beginnings of a mustache and whiskers are growing on his muscular face.

"It's more people getting killed by people than people trying to commit suicide."

"That's true." Marie joins the conversation. "They could have done their tape on anything. And this was the topic that we chose. And the reason that they chose it was because there were several people who suggested it in a way that was very powerful." Marie turns to Monica and Majandra. "Do you guys feel like talking to Jonathan? Because he doesn't understand why we're doing this topic." She also turns to Jonathan to suggest he learn more about the subject.

He continues to argue loudly with Marie. "I don't have to read nothin'. Especially on a topic like this. Suicide is sick! You know what I'm saying? To prevent suicide. You shouldn't even think like that! That's not reality. Yo."

"You have to be respectful of other folks' perspectives. But I think it is great that you are here with a completely different point of view."

"I'm sayin', when we present this to the school. When we present this to the school, people are gonna look at the whole class as being crazy. 'Cause that's a crazy topic, suicide."

Christina and Marie's strategy is to remove Jonathan from the class and engage him with Majandra. He might feel less angry and less threatened if another student can humanize the subject. So, eventually, Jonathan is persuaded to go to the principal's office with Majandra. Not because they are in trouble, but because that is where there is a telephone that they can use. Their assignment is to begin the research process by calling hospitals, to set up interviews with psychiatrists.

Majandra and Jonathan sit down in the office as Marie goes to get information on who to call. No one else is there, just the three of us, and the red and black poster of Che Guevara on the wall. I situate myself between them, point the camera at Jonathan, and ask, "What is it that bothers you most about doing this topic?"

"It's not relevant to me."

"It's not relevant? What would have been a more relevant topic for you?"

"I don't know, like, like I'm saying. People starving. Homelessness. There's more people starvin'. That's a slow death. That more horrible than killin' yourself. They fightin' for meals. People that's homeless . . ."

"So that would be a topic you wanted to look at?"

"I'm saying, it's not that I want a look at, 'cause I see that, I look at that every day. I see that every day around me . . . Suicide, that's like, something that's evil. How you gonna kill yourself when there's so much to live for? So much opportunity, so much space, air, fresh air. You know what I'm saying. Why would you wanna kill yourself?"

I pan over to Majandra. She is hanging her head a bit, staring blankly ahead. She is rubbing her lips together as if she has just put on Chapstick.

Training the camera on her, I expect she will understand the cue and begin to speak. But she says nothing. I decide to risk creating a potentially confrontational situation and prompt her to respond to Jonathan's statement. "Do you think it's evil? Do you agree with what he is saying?"

She turns to me and smiles nervously. An answer begins to form. "I mean, basically . . . you see, a person who is going through it, doesn't think about not coming back, doesn't think about the fresh air around and everything. There's like no time to think." Sunlight coming in from the window in the back of the office illuminates her face. Her hair coming down half covers her right eye.

> The only thing you're thinking about, 'cause the only thing I was thinking about, was everything bad going on around me. If you were thinking about the bright side, then you wouldn't want to do it. A lot of people are so depressed that they're not thinking about nothing bright. They only think about what is wrong, and that is why you think about doing it . . . I mean I had a lot of reasons for doing it. I personally, thinking back about it, didn't really wanna die.

Her mouth turns down in an ugly frown as she almost spits out the words 'wanna die.'

"I was thinking about death at that moment. . . . It, it, . . . Phewww! It's too much. It's too much for me right now . . ."

"It's better things to think about than that . . . You too pretty. Yo, you shouldn't think like that. You young. You aint payin' no bills . . ." Jonathan is into a rhythm, slapping his fist in his hand to punctuate his statements. "Once you get your education and diploma you gonna have so much opportunities and stuff . . ."

> "I do great around here," says Majandra. "Around here, normally I show people that I'm happy. When I'm at home, I used to be at home arguing with my parents every day. Arguing with my family every day. Arguing with my friends every day. Dealing with all kinds of crap. You know what I'm saying? I had to run away from home. I had to move out of the house and go with my grandmother because of all that . . . I didn't wanna deal with nobody no more, 'cause if nobody cares about me, why should I care about me? I did it real stupid. I drank a whole bottle of Dimetapp. Almost passed out. I called my cousin before I did and told her good-bye on the voice mail."

She covers her face with her hands. Then she drops them in her lap. Now they are up again, this time with her fingers slightly spread out, just touching the side of her face up to her temples. "Yo, when I was in that hospital, I felt like a freakin' lunatic. The people took me. They put me in the room." Her pace quickens. "They made me change my clothes, put on hospitals clothes, took my shoelaces off. They thought I was gonna tie the shoelace up and hang myself!" She catches her breath and ties an imaginary rope around her neck.

After this emotionally draining experience, we make our way back to the rest of the class. We never make the telephone calls. It turns out that Marie had decided not to interrupt us and had made the calls to the hospital herself.

Jonathan is no longer visibly angry and resistant. He is ready and able to be a part of the group. In fact, later that afternoon, he practiced interviewing Majandra on camera. He also practiced directing other students to shoot the camera and conduct interviews.

Maybe it was because he was given the opportunity to have his say, to voice his concerns and fears. He could buy into the class project because he could come to terms with it and make it his own. It no longer seemed as threatening to participate in a project about suicide; maybe the fear that he would somehow be humiliated or thought to be crazy by the rest of the school no longer seemed as real.

Maybe it was the face-to-face exchange with a classmate that humanized the thing he said was evil. Letting Majandra tell her story and offering praise and advice, in whatever way he could, was perhaps what broadened his understanding and made possible empathy for the person as separate from the act she attempted.

My presence was an important factor in shaping the exchange that took place. I had assumed multiple roles during the conversation, at times as a probing researcher, manipulative provocateur, concerned video teacher, interested outsider, social worker, and silent witness. And what about the camera? What role did it play? Would the exact same exchange have taken place if I weren't videotaping it? Did the camera bring me more authority and so command a performance of moralizing speeches and passionate testimonials from the students that would never have taken place otherwise? Did it diminish the authenticity of the encounter, or did it simply make it possible?

## INTERVIEWING

*I'm not like those other interviewers. Interviewers, they read their little papers with questions. I don't do that. I freestyle.*—Julius

In her work with nonmainstream students, Shirley Brice Heath found that they were able to develop literacies of the dominant culture by practicing ethnographic kinds of research in their own community, through a kind of apprenticeship with the teacher. It required close guidance in a group-learning environment with an emphasis on the role of imitation and observation and always contextualization. This approach helped students practice in a meaningful context the various subskills of essay-text literacy, such as asking questions and note-taking. Heath (1983) wrote:

> Gathering information from observers of their own participation in reading and writing, they had verified skills of theirs which were not being measured by school tests . . . In short, what their central lesson had been: it is important for a person to know what he is doing when he uses language. If one uses a dialect form, one should know why. If one uses a casual style, one does so in relation to the occasion and the listener. (pp. 333–334)

As Gee (1996) noted:

> The component skills of this form of literacy must be practiced, one cannot practice a skill one has not been exposed to, cannot engage in a social practice one has not been socialized into, which is what most non-mainstream children are expected to do in school. (p. 65)

Over the semester, Marie worked with Christina to provide the students with a range of opportunities to analyze and practice the subskills that were embedded in documentary production. This was the cognitive and affective scaffolding needed to build the more complex skills that come under the heading of research, interviewing, editing, and camera work. Writing was woven into all activities. Even calling prospective subjects on the telephone to arrange for interviews was a skill that needed development. Regardless if the students were verbal or not, they lacked experience in this kind of talk. As Monica explained, "I wouldn't know how to talk a person, unless I'm crank calling them." When asked if it made a difference whether she talked with an adult or a young person, she answered, "Yeah, it does. 'Cause I usually don't talk to adults. I talk to young people."

To monitor their development, students each kept portfolios and collected samples of work in these areas. They eventually selected one area of specialization in preparation for the presentation they would have to give before the portfolio committee at the end of the semester.

## Learning to Interview

Christina and Marie spent more time developing the students' interviewing skills than on any other area. On several occasions, they facilitated practice interview activities where the students would take turns shooting, conducting, and critiquing interviews, as the following section illustrates.

In this case the two students are seated facing each other. They look small. Maybe it is because they only fill the lower half of screen. The white board behind them takes up the upper half. There is way too much headroom. The camera is shooting down on them from above. And what they are saying is barely audible. Maybe there is something wrong with the mic or the audio cable. The sound needs to be turned up higher on the monitor to hear them.

Holding the mic to his mouth, Jonathan looks into the camera and says, "Hello, East City High School, this is Jonathan and Majandra doing an interview about teen suicide and how to prevent it, for 2000. All right."

With a bit of swagger and a swivel, he turns to face Majandra and asks, "Hello, Majandra. How you doing?" He glances down at the paper in his lap. "Can I ask you, if it's not too personal, have you ever thought about committing suicide?"

"Yes, I have."

"Can I ask you what made you think about it?"

Her face grows larger in the frame as the camera zooms into a close-up. Actually, the profile shot only captures some of her face, since her hair is covering much of it. She tells her story.

Marie stops the tape. She is teaching a lesson on interviewing to one group of students. She wants them to focus on what the interviewer is doing to guide the conversation. The rest of the class is sitting with Christina on the other side of the room, analyzing elements of the visual language in the video footage they had shot, such as the framing, angles, and movement of the camera.

"We need to figure out what is being done right and what needs some improvement," explains Marie. "Because I think most of these we are going to redo. Everyone should have out paper and pencil for this. Three of you look for the things that are strong in the interview, that are good, and two of you look for things that need improvement."

After writing their observations for a few moments, Crystal raises her hand. "He said, 'If it's not too personal.'"

Majandra laughs, "Yeah, I liked that."

"You did appreciate that when you were going through it?" Marie echoes as she goes to the board to write. "So, he asked, 'If it's not too personal?' How can I word that to put it on our list? If we are telling people advice on doing interviews? Something you should do is what?"

Gail responds, "Always, if you feel that a question is personal, ask them if it is too personal. Ask them if you could ask them a personal question."

Majandra adds, "He started by saying, 'Hi, how are you.' He started with a greeting. I thought that was nice . . . There was another thing that made me more comfortable. He was actually paying attention to what I was saying."

"That's good. So how should we word that for our list?"

"He took interest in her feelings."

"Try to take interest. Use body language to show you are taking interest in the subject."

"Okay, take interest. And what kind of body language would that be?" Marie asks.

"Nod your head. Make eye contact."

Julius had a different approach. He had declared his interest in interviewing early and often. He said he had never interviewed anyone before this class and was proud to show off this newfound skill he never knew he had. As he described it, he was best at interviewing people "freestyle." By this, he meant an improvisational, unstructured form of conversation not based on a preplanned set of questions. "I come to you and ask questions that come to my mind . . . I just go with the flow. I ask a question. If the answer consists of the question, then I ask another question. Then I ask another one. That's just really my style. I know most people, my teachers don't like my style. But my style's a free style."

Julius was aware that his "freestyle" approach to interviewing ran counter to what Christina and Marie were trying to teach the class. His strategy was free both in terms of it being improvisational and also in terms of being free of paper. He relied on his memory, without having to write or read anything. He was not alone in declaring his strong preference for the freestyle approach. Several students in the EVC *Young Gunz* project had wanted to improvise rather than be confined to a written structure.

Of course, the teachers emphasized using writing to support and guide the interview process. Questions had to be written down and then accessed casually, to direct but not to interrupt the flow of conversation. In addition, research informed some of the questions being written. This required even more reading and writing.

Julius's interest in the improvisational approach to interviewing is understandable. First, there is a strong presence of improvisation in genres of youth culture such as hip-hop music, poetry slams, dance, jazz, and other art forms, including the art of conversation. Improvisation also seems to be the chosen form of discourse used in the most popular and visible genres of interviewing that teenagers watch on television: sports, talk shows, and MTV. The interviewer runs onto the field just after the team wins the championship and seems to say whatever is on his or her mind. There is no paper or writing visible anywhere. The same is true of the questions posed to the rap star who just won a Grammy Award, or of David Letterman's offhand banter with his guests. It all appears to be spontaneous and free-flowing.

What is not visible is years of practice and the structured work (written, musical, and otherwise) that was done prior to the moment of public performance to make the improvisation possible. This is part of what Marie and Christina were trying to help Julius and the other students realize and accomplish.

When Julius first began conducting interviews for the suicide video, his television-influenced freestyle approach was very evident. He adopted the verbal and body language of a television news correspondent, or at least how he imagined a television reporter would speak and act. This may have been because it was the discourse with which he was familiar, or because it lent him more prestige and credibility than simply being a student from a video class, or both. But over three takes with two different students he worked from memory to perfect his introduction. This was his way of including his own beliefs about the causes of suicide and, specifically, the issue he had wanted to pursue instead of suicide: peer pressure.

His first interview begins with a close-up on him, looking straight into the camera. He is wearing a black do-rag and a blue Yankees vest over a white t-shirt.

"Yeah, yo, what's up. This is East City News with Julius Smith. We doing an interview about suicide. And um, I have a guest here, Gail." The camera pans left to a medium shot of Gail. Then it zooms out to a wide angle. The two of them are seated in the hallway.

"And, um . . . I'm about to just go down with the interview." He points the mic toward her. "What do you think about when you hear the word 'suicide'?"

"I think about people that I know that tried to commit suicide."

"Yeah, awright, and what, what situation might, might you—damn!"

He throws out his arm in disgust, making a swift cutting motion with his hand holding the mic. The camera cuts.

The shot zooms out to a wide angle of Julius sitting with another student in the same hallway. "Yeah, what's up. This is East City News. This is Julius Smith. We doing an interview about suicide. Now, as we know, suicide is a big issue during the teen years. For example, peer pressure, family issues, and other issues as well. So now we got a little—Damn!" He doubles over in his chair and signals for the camera to cut again.

When he interviewed a student from another class in the school some weeks later, his tone and body language had changed. He no longer tried to mimic the conventions of TV news programs. Perhaps he was feeling more comfortable with alternative conventions that might be more appropriate to a PBS talk show or a documentary production. Another shift in the conventions used was the framing of this interview. The camera stayed focused on the student being interviewed. Julius was not on camera at all. Instead of emphasizing the identification of himself and an imaginary news show, he signaled a more serious tone by thanking the interviewee for being there and shaking his hand. It may also have been a sign of respect because this interview subject was a male.

A medium shot shows a serious-looking boy sitting with a wood closet behind him. He is wearing a blue ski jacket.

"All right. Thanks for coming. Do you have any past history dealing with suicide?" The camera zooms into a close-up.

"Yes, I have. Actually, a friend of mine committed suicide. It was like the week, a day or two after midterms week. And we were all stressed out. We were all drinking. Stupid thing to do. He was, like, kinda drunk. He was dishing out problems with his mom and his dad. He was a really wealthy kid. But, I don't know. He popped eight aspirins in his room by himself upstairs followed by a bottle of vodka. When we got there, it was too late. I tried to get him to vomit and my friend Ian tried to get the ambulance. But, since we were in a boarding school in Connecticut in the country, it took too long for the ambulance to get there. And he died in the ambulance on the way to the hospital."

Julius followed that unexpected answer with an appropriate sign of sympathy, "I'm sorry to hear that . . ." Then he integrated information he had gathered through research into a question: "As his friend, what do you think about from past histories and information that boys commit suicide a little bit more than girls? What is your insight on that one?" He switched his form of questioning to a conversational yet directive prompt: "So, tell us, what is your message to other teenagers around here that's thinking this situation like your friend did?" Eliciting a message for young viewers shifts Julius's role from a disengaged news or sports reporter to a more activist, community-minded or public service kind of journalist. And finally, he ends the interview with a respectful, professional, and confident close: "All right, thanks for having you." His hand enters the frame to shake the interviewee's hand. "It was good having you. And thanks for telling us about your story. Thanks." Fade to black.

Later in the week Christina screens this interview for the entire class. She uses it to reinforce the skills of logging, interviewing, and self-evaluation.

"Julius, this is your area of interest, right? Interviewing? This could be a base point for you. If you wanted to really evaluate yourself . . . You really need to look at this closely. How are you going to choose what you did well, and what you . . . you know, weed out, what worked the best? How are you going to do that?"

"I gotta look at the tape again, 'cause I don't really remember all, every single one of my questions that I asked."

"So take notes, right? You are going to look at it and you are going to stop it when you need to. . . . What made his interview special? It wasn't what you expected, right?"

"It really happened to him."

"He had a real experience. How did you find that out?"

"I asked him questions, 'Do he have any past history with the subject?'"

"There you go. That was a good question, 'cause you got way more than you bargained for, right?"

"The problem is, I freestyled it. And I didn't write it down. So now I don't really remember it."

"But you have it. See, this is your notes. Right here. You can look at it. You can look at it as many times as you want. . . . This is really a piece for you to use, Julius, for your portfolio. Then you can evaluate yourself, Julius."

Julius seems to be struggling with the limits of his memory. It is as if he is expected to remember everything that was said in the interview—all his questions and all the answers—and admits he can't. He freestyled it. He hasn't written them down. He doesn't think of video as a form of visual and aural notation that he can refer back to until Christina makes it clear to him. There seems to be a shift of sorts in his thinking. Video becomes a record, a tool, an aid to his memory, not simply a source of entertainment. But to make full use of this tool, as Christina points out, he has to use another form of recordkeeping, another aid to memory: writing.

## REFLECTIONS AND RELEASES

*Basically, it improved skills I never knew I had. Like interviewing. It basically helped me have a way of speaking.*—Julius

Through their project, the students interviewed students in their class and in other classes of the school, as well as school psychologists and hospital-based psychiatrists. They also conducted some limited research from books, newspaper articles, and video documentaries; wrote and read poems; wrote and performed skits; recorded music; taped artwork they had painted; and edited the material together. So what sorts of new skills and knowledge did the students develop through all this activity? And how can we measure this kind of learning?

When Julius was asked if his writing skills improved any as a result of his video work, he responded, "We sure write a lot. I don't know if I improved it. Basically, it improved skills I never knew I had. Like interviewing. It basically helped me have a way of speaking. . . . It taught me better how to speak as well as writing."

He explained that one of the reasons he liked the video class was because he learns best by talking, and it gave him a chance to do what he was good at. "I'm not good at tests. With tests, I just suck up. I get scared and fail the tests. I like to learn by doing my work, homework, class work, or talking . . . I learn better by talking, I don't like to write."

In comparing his work on the first class project, "East City Dreams," with the more extensive documentary on suicide entitled "Flirting with Death," he observed that the latter was more difficult since it required him to do more research and conduct more serious interviews:

> With *Dreams*, I was laid back. I was asking questions: "How was your dreams? How was your obstacles to your dreams?" I could understand dreams. Everybody have dreams. You didn't have to know the history of dreams. Suicide is kinda hard, 'cause I had to actually interview people who actually tried to kill themselves. It's kinda hard. . . . I didn't really understand: Why would people wanna kill themselves? . . . So I had to be a little bit sensitive with

> my questions, instead of having fun. I got to get a straight face on. Part of it is the people I got to talk to and part of it is the technical stuff. The research and all that. Reading those articles . . . You got to look at papers. A whole bunch of research.

Reflecting on the last interview he did, Julius said,

> This was a different interview because it was a little bit emotional. 'Cause the person I interviewed lost a friend by the subject of suicide. And it was a lot emotional. And basically, it was a surprise for me when I asked him what's his past history about suicide and he said he lost a friend by it. It was real emotional. It was a real shock for me. It basically made me get a little bit sensitive about the person I was asking questions to.

Julius learned to shift his discourse, his way of talking and acting, to meet this social interaction. As he put it, he learned to "get a straight face on."

In his Interviewing Portfolio cover letter, he wrote: "What made me learn about interviewing was another documentary called 'Flirting with Death' and what I have improved in this was my questions. They were more clear and I really didn't free speak. Plus I showed a lot of improvement of being serious into my work."

Julius's recognition that he had to be more serious in his video work had broader implications beyond the video class. In his portfolio presentation for his American Literature class, Christina reported that he made the connection between Ralph Ellison's *Invisible Man* and his own sense of identity. "The thing that was so great, was that he tied this in to his own personal identity. He connected them thematically. He said he had been a lazy person. When he came into video art, he felt it was going to be easy. He finally realized that it was important to do his work. He had to sit down and think about the kind of questions he had to ask. He asked deeper questions. This was work. He learned that he, Julius, could work. This was a revelation for him. He was proud of himself. Because of the seriousness of the topic, he had to be thoughtful. He couldn't just blast away with whatever was on the top of his head. It made him become more serious as a worker and a student. He connected that with his own self-identity, as a hard worker and as a competent student."

His English teacher, who also attended his portfolio presentation, noted how the medium of video literally made visible the problems and the progress in his work. It made self-reflection and self-critique more accessible. "Viewing his work and seeing how inadequate it was, was important. He saw it immediately on video. But he couldn't see it in his writing. He saw immediately how he could improve."

Jonathan wrote in his Portfolio cover letter,

> During the course of the year other students and myself have been working on tapes about two topics Dreams and Suicide. For our last project, we made a documentary about suicide. At first, I didn't want to do this project because I felt it was boring, but after I heard stories this made me understand how serious the topic is. People that are teenagers and adults suffer from this illness. So what I did was I wanted to learn about preventions centers to understand how I can help people from taking their life.

Shaniqua wrote,

> My area of expertise was in editing . . . My reasons for choosing editing were because editors have all the control. We chose what to cut and what stays. Editing gives you a lot of power. Even though it gives you complete power there is still hard work involved. . . . It is important to have a flow through your tape. My way of creating a flow is by thinking about something I would say and trying to have the tape speak the same way, have the tape express my opinions and others. Editing is very time consuming—but it's rewarding to me watching a complete tape and knowing that I had a big part in putting it together.

By mid-June the students were almost finished editing the project and were preparing for their portfolio presentations. Christina, Marie, and I all agreed that we needed to have Majandra's parents sign a release for her, since she was the most prominent student to have her suicide story told in the tape. I also needed her parents to sign a release to use her interviews for this book. Her mother told me she would sign the release. I went with Majandra to meet her mother in her apartment after school the next day, but to my surprise, she had changed her mind. She explained that Majandra's father had vetoed the idea. This was very disturbing news for Majandra and for me. After some discussion, we agreed to all meet at the school the next day to resolve the matter.

When I arrived, both Majandra's mother and her father were on one side of the table in the art room and Majandra, Christina, and Marie were on the other side. Both of her parents were wearing East City Little League t-shirts. Christina was explaining what the class project was about, and I began to add to it. Majandra's father was stone-faced. When he spoke, he explained that he mainly was interested in Majandra's future. It's nice to make a tape that can help others who may be depressed or suicidal, he said, but he was concerned about her. How would speaking out in this tape affect her future career? Would others use it against her? How would the other kids in school treat her?

Majandra got visibly agitated at this. "But I told the truth about what happened to me and I didn't say anything about you two," she insisted. "I am just talking about me. And I am not the only one with this problem. There are millions and millions of others who also attempted suicide. But they don't have anyone to talk to about it."

"I know there are millions of others," he responded. "But you are my only daughter. I am concerned about you."

Then the East City High School principal joined us. He said he had to leave to go to another meeting, but he was thinking about this and just wanted to add a few things. First, he said it was a family decision, but as a community we would help give them other perspectives on the subject. Ultimately, it was the family that had to decide. Also, he said he understood what they were going through because he had had a somewhat analogous experience as a recovering alcoholic and drug addict—personal information that he had not wanted to share. But he later found out that talking about it helped him come to terms with his problems and made him a stronger person. It also provided hope for others to see how he had turned his life around. It was certainly not an easy decision. There are things you give up and things you gain, he said.

Majandra's father repeated his concerns. And he said that he and his wife also both had drug and alcohol problems they were recovering from. But they wanted to make sure that in the future, if Majandra was making her career as a journalist, it wouldn't be used against her, like the way Vanessa Williams's nude photos caused her to lose her Miss America crown. Majandra assured him that she had done all her interviews with her clothes on.

I felt that it was important for them to see what the tapes were about. I told them that Majandra was quite eloquent; that the students really responded to their peers and that they would really listen to what she had to say. And far from feeling ashamed, she would later look back on the tape and what she had accomplished and would feel proud.

Marie showed the opening three or four minutes of the tape that had already been edited. Then we all turned to Majandra's father.

He started to talk slowly. He said there was nothing there that he saw that he felt he would prevent from being shown. It was really up to Majandra. It is her life and it is her decision, he said. He would not disagree with any of it. There was a collective sigh of relief on our side of the table. I tried not to show my sense of excitement. Christina thanked him. I spoke to him about how other kids who have gone out on a limb making tapes about community and personal issues have actually won festival awards and scholarships.

After a while, just as we were getting ready to go, Majandra's father said, "You know, I never saw it coming. I had no idea that she wanted to kill herself. That the problem was so bad. You never see the parents' point of view."

Majandra said, "Well, let's get out the camera." I thought she was joking and that her father would immediately get up and walk out. But he stayed. He wanted to talk. He had a story to tell. Marie and I looked at each other; I grabbed a camera case and began to open it. Majandra wrote down a couple of questions on a big sheet of drawing paper that was lying around (we were in Christina's art room). Majandra's father had one request, that the name "EAST CITY LITTLE LEAGUE" on his t-shirt would not be in the picture. The request was granted, and the interview was shot in a close-up.

The camera was a three-quarter shot of Majandra's father. He was facing toward the right side of the screen. The mic was coming out of the lower right corner. His hair was cut short. His face was round, youthful, kind, but serious. His blue t-shirt blended into the bright blue wall of the art room.

> "Hi, my name is Majandra and I'm here interviewing my father on teen suicide. Did you see—wait, first of all. Hi, how you doing?"
>
> "I'm okay," he said softly, smiling awkwardly out of the side of his mouth. He looked down.
>
> "Did you see any signs of suicide in me before I decided to attempt suicide?"
>
> "No, I didn't see any signs. You know. As a parent, you just, you just, I don't know what you're thinking. You just expect your kid to take everything in stride and move along. As a parent, you never expect *your* kid to do something like that, it's always someone else's kid. You know? It was hard to accept when I found out. After you find out, then you start asking yourself questions like what part did I play in it? And, what could I have done to prevent it?"
>
> "How did you feel when you found out that I had attempted suicide?"
>
> "Again, I was shocked. I thought it was some kind of mistake. That it wasn't you . . . On my way to the hospital all I could think about was, you know, what have I done so bad that you would

attempt suicide? I know that we had our problems. That you had a hard time accepting my personal problems. Which have nothing to do with you." He wiped his nose, choked on his words, and lost his voice for a moment. "But they do impact you. That is one of the mistakes I made is to mini—you know, not realize the whole impact of my personal problems on your life."

"If you could turn back time, what would you have done to make things different?"

"You know, there are so many things. You know, I could have straightened out my own life, and encouraged you. I think the biggest thing is to encourage your kid to talk to you. Talk to their parents. Not create an atmosphere of fear. That, if you would come up to me with some issue or something and be fearful that I would be screaming and yelling, which is things that I do. That I've done. And, if a kid can't communicate with your parent, it is very important. Go to your best friend. Don't do anything drastic. . . . You can't fix things by, by committing suicide. You know, if you love the people, who supposedly are not loving you back, it is devastating to the people you leave behind. That's another thing I was thinking. What if she would have been successful? What was I gonna—How was I going to live the rest of my life? You know? Not only your life would have ended right there. You know. Many people's lives would have ended right there." He looked away, then glanced quickly at Majandra, then looked down at the floor.

"Okay. This is Majandra signing off." She tried to choke back her tears, but they streamed down her face anyway.

This was an authentic exhibition, a demonstration of lessons learned unlike any other I had seen. Majandra had worked hard to apply her interviewing skills in this situation: to develop questions that can elicit the answers you are looking for, to be polite, engaged, and professional. But the object of the interview was also the active subject conducting the interview. She was both the writer and the narrative being written. She had never had this conversation with her father before; it was somehow only made possible with the aid of the camera.

This is Majandra's Portfolio letter:

> For this class my area of expertise is interviewing. I chose interviewing because I feel it will help me in the field of journalism. This is a field that I would like to pursue in the future.
>
> To analyze my area of expertise I chose the interview I did with my father . . . I feel that my body language was good. I didn't

> ask too many questions, but I asked the right questions to get his point of view on his suicidal teen across.
>
> . . . What I leaned about my area of expertise while doing this interview had nothing to do with body language or the proper questions. I learned that doing a personal interview is harder than any interview possible. It is hard being professional when you are the person being discussed on the other end of the table. The interview between my father and me was extremely hard because it was very emotional and personal for me.
>
> The thing that I learned about this interview most of all was that my father actually does care about me. And I learned exactly how he felt about my experience with suicide. I enjoyed doing this interview and I learned something that will last me a lifetime in three questions.

A week later, we talked about the interview with her father. I asked whether she was surprised that her father wanted to talk with her.

"At first I was. Yeah, I was surprised more at what he said more than the fact he wanted to say it."

"Why did that surprise you?"

"'Cause I didn't know how he felt. He didn't tell me. We don't get to discuss things like that all the time. And I learned."

"Why do you think he only told you when he was on camera in front of other people?"

"I don't know. I guess that was the opportunity for us to talk. Because when we are not on camera . . . we don't listen to each other. That was a moment in time where I had to listen. I had no choice but to listen. So he said what he had to say."

"You said it was very difficult doing that interview with your father?"

"Yeah, I didn't think it was going to be difficult at first but it ended up difficult while I was sitting there and I started crying. I mean, 'cause it's not very professional. Barbara Walters doesn't cry during her interviews."

"You were trying to be professional."

"Yeah, but you can't, in situations like that. It's really hard. And I guess that's why they don't let Barbara Walters interview her parents."

## TRANSFORMATIONS

The video class was a transformational experience for the students, and in Majandra's case, for her parents as well. It took the students on a startling journey that challenged them to struggle with new skills, ideas, and ways of knowing themselves and each other. They grew intellectually and emotionally through that struggle, although they each found different entry points into the project and took different paths of learning. While conventional academic teaching strives for uniformity—all students studying the same subject at the same time, and drawing the same lessons from it—part of the richness of the video inquiry was that it engaged students in such a diversity of experiences, allowing them each to grow in their own way.

Julius came to see himself as a more capable and self-reflective student, able to interview his peers about the most serious of subjects with both skill and sensitivity. Jonathan developed a sense of empathy for people struggling with depression and suicide where he had once felt only fear and anger. Majandra became more self-confident both as an interviewer and the subject of interviews, proud that she could publicly tell her story though video, and that it might help other kids facing similar problems. And as she noted, it was her interview with her father—as hard as it was for her to conduct—where she learned the real strength of her skill, courage, and poise as a young journalist. It was also where she learned how much her father really cared for her.

When asked how they might teach the class differently next time, both Christina and Marie were full of ideas, including restructuring how they used the class time and focusing more on print literacy skills. Christina felt that she still needed more practice with the video equipment and more experience in facilitating group project work.

More experienced educators would undoubtedly find this to be a powerful way of teaching, but they, too, would need to work through and find balance in some of its inherent tensions. For example, the students were engaged by the immediacy of the personal and social issues that they explored, but it was the closeness of the subject matter that could also push them away. The collaborative nature of the video project enabled the students to work as interdependent learners, at various time collaborating, teaching, and learning from each other. But building and maintaining a cohesive group out of a collection of individual students requires skilled facilitation and daily care and attention. Working in the medium of video enabled the students' inner thoughts, questions, and stories to be externalized as a product that could be exhibited to public audiences with pride. But too much emphasis on the end product could also eclipse the importance of the process, causing students to view their mistakes along the way as a mark of failure instead of as important opportunities for reflection and learning.

Without question, this is hard work; good teaching always is. But the payoff for that work was not only in the skills and sense of accomplishment that the students began to develop, but also in the opportunity it gave them to talk openly about what were literally life-and-death issues for them. Refusing to respect the segregation of intellect from emotion that most schools enforce, this class turned the emotional problem of teen depression and suicide into the object of study and turned academic study into an emotionally engaging experience. They made discoveries about themselves and each other that would not otherwise have been possible. And so, by sharing and listening to the stories of despair that so many teens carry inside every day in school, the students learned to explore deeper levels of truth and hope.

CHAPTER 4

# *Conclusion: Reimagining the School Day*

THE DOCUMENTARY-MAKING PROCESS gave the East City High School students something they rarely found at school or elsewhere in their lives: a visible victory. Unlike so many of their other experiences at home and in school, which ended in disappointment and failure, this class yielded tangible evidence that they could succeed, that if they stuck with a project over time their hard work would pay off. With their video, the students could literally show off their ideas and creativity to teachers, family, friends, neighbors, and whomever else they could get to watch it.

But as rich as their experience was, the use of video inquiry as a methodology for teaching and learning did not become institutionalized as part of the school's culture. As was the case with most other schools in which the Educational Video Center has worked, media education remained the province of individual teachers who, as popular as they may be with their following of students, usually ended up working in isolation from their colleagues.

This pattern of effective but isolated use was not unique to East City. It is a problem that is larger than any one school or district. The community-based and learner-centered approach to media education has failed to fit into the underlying purposes and structures of school as a national institution.

This chapter takes a step back from the particular case studies of EVC student work to look more generally at new strategies and possibilities that are emerging for media education within the movement of after-school programs and community–school collaborations. In looking at the broader context of EVC's work, I discuss recent efforts to reimagine the school day for urban kids, which I believe can create opportunities to connect and bring relevance to their varied experiences of school, mass media culture, and community life. I also examine some of the institutional barriers that have frustrated our efforts to integrate media analysis and production into schools.

Of particular interest is the growing convergence among the fields of education, youth development, and community development. This movement is bringing teachers, youth workers, and community activists together to reimagine how they can support the intellectual, creative, and civic organizing capacities of young people while at the same time rebuilding their ravaged communities. Professional development for teachers and program staff is increasingly stressed as being key to this effort.

However, what is generally missing from these collaborative efforts is the inclusion of media literacy and media production as significant components of youth learning and community activity. For this reason, media educators need to be part of the conversation and part of the planning, for they have much to gain, and certainly much to contribute.

## BARRIERS IN SCHOOL

To build a strategy for both deepening and broadening the impact of youth media work, it is important to better understand some of the bureaucratic and pedagogical roadblocks on both the state and local levels to integrating media education into school curricula. Among them are problems of teacher certification, professional development, testing requirements, and scheduling.

State departments of education do not recognize media literacy or media education as a discrete subject area in which states award licenses to teachers or administer standardized tests to students. Therefore, faculty are not trained to teach students to analyze and produce media, nor are such classes mandated as part of students' coursework. Interested teachers must pick up the skills on their own or through in-service courses, and then negotiate with colleagues and administrators for the time and space to teach media within discrete subject areas such as English, social studies, or art; as an elective; or outside of the school day altogether, as an after-school club. The national trend toward high-stakes testing is forcing schools to set aside more time for test preparation in core subject areas, and reduce time for innovative classes outside the core subject areas.

The scheduling and structure of most schools also creates a number of other obstacles. The 50-minute periods that mark off the day in most high schools make it virtually impossible for students to become engaged in in-depth projects that routinely take them outside the school walls. Academic credit is often not granted to students for coursework that doesn't fit into mandated subject areas. The interdisciplinary nature of media education classes makes it difficult for schools to departmentalize the work. Finally, the limited time and funds for professional development in most school districts undercuts the ongoing support that they need to develop a broad repertoire of group facilitation and counseling, social journalism, and technical video skills.

These problems stem in part from negative perceptions that permeate both the local and state levels of education policymakers. To bring media into the classroom as a serious subject of study, they must overcome the view that since video is a close relative of television, it can only be a source of distraction and entertainment for students. Devoid of those academic rituals that supposedly give a subject its weight and rigor, such as tests, book reports, and nightly homework assignments, media education has not been considered to be academically serious subject matter. In the common vocabulary of education, schooling, literacy, and the printed word are still woven together as tightly as rope. So when one speaks of teaching visual literacy, juxtaposing language and images, it is as if one is tearing one fiber apart from the other, threatening to cause the whole thing to unravel.

Confining youth media to the margins of schools greatly reduces the scope and impact the field can potentially have on young people nationally. While some practitioners may say that this marginalization frees them to be more independent and innovative, I would argue that the lack of institutional support and stable funding has stunted the overall growth of the field; youth media organizations that are perpetually consumed with the immediate business of survival are hard pressed to build their long-term capacity and deepen their work. Furthermore, working outside of mainstream structures risks isolating youth media efforts from the communities they are designed to serve.

Clearly, the factory model of school must be radically reformed in order for a rigorous media education program to become an integral part of school life, especially an innovation such as EVC's, which transgresses so many established boundaries. This is even becoming the case with small and alternative schools, which, despite their struggles to break free of that model, are increasingly being forced to comply with its testing and curricular requirements.

School reform efforts continue to go on in virtually every big city in the country, but it is slow and painstaking work. And so media education practitioners must either join forces with education reformers or look outside of schools to find other institutional partners. EVC has chosen to follow both strategies.

## OPPORTUNITIES AFTER SCHOOL

While general reliance on the old factory model of education has created an unsupportive environment for community-based media education, the field of after-school programs has been more accommodating. In addition to offering fewer bureaucratic restrictions and a closer connection to the local neighborhood, community youth service agencies such as YMCAs, Boys and Girls Clubs, and the Children's Aid Society are among the many networks of organizations that can partner with, strengthen, and potentially scale up the work of youth media groups nationally.

The experiences of EVC and other youth media organizations have shown that many after-school programs offer a range of approaches and beliefs that, unlike traditional schools, are congruent with and creates openings for such work. These include a more holistic approach that addresses the social, emotional, creative, and cognitive needs of teenagers; an asset-based perspective that focuses on youth strengths and promotes youth voices in decision-making; a commitment to engaging youth in service to their local community; a flexibility in both scheduling and content of youth activities; and a relative freedom from the requirements of standardized academic testing. The implementation of these beliefs is uneven, depending in part on the available resources and experienced staff a particular program has.

After-school programs have enjoyed unprecedented growth in recent years, particularly in low-income urban communities. Policymakers, practitioners, and philanthropists see such programs as an effective way to accomplish a variety of goals, including meeting children's needs for safe environments and supervision from caring adults while their parents are working; bolstering academic achievement; supporting overall youth development; and supporting youth engagement in community development. These community-based programs have come to occupy what has been called the "third arena," a time and place in between school and family where children can learn and grow (Kangisser, 1999).

Some broad social and economic developments affecting low-income children and teenagers underlie this growing trend. Prompted in part by the welfare reform laws that have pushed large numbers of poor women into the job market, now more school-age children have parents who work outside the home. An estimated five to seven million, and up to as many as 15 million, "latchkey children" return to an empty home after school (Chung, 2000).

After-school programs also address the needs of young adults in the transitional years between ages 17 and 23. Those who are out of high school, not in college, and unemployed become more alienated from their communities just at the time when they are provided with fewer supports and opportunities than younger teens to become engaged in structured community activities and leadership experiences. Research has shown that as youth get older, the number of young adults who are disengaged from their community increases. The more disengaged they are from the community, the more likely they are to end up in the juvenile justice system (Irby, Ferber, & Pitman, 2001).

Many after-school programs initially grew out of community development projects aimed at developing jobs, affordable housing, and quality health care, but the field has now become even more diverse. It includes traditional before- and after-school programs, summer camps, tutoring and mentoring programs, cultural and arts activities, clubs, and lessons. After-school programs can also vary in schedule, from drop-in to full-time enrollment programs. Furthermore, many types of institutions, including nonprofit groups, community agencies, faith-based institutions, and public and private schools, operate after-school programs (Halpern, Deich, & Cohen, 2000).

EVC's approach to media education can play a much-needed role in furthering the multiple purposes of after-school programs. Community documentary projects develop kids' literacy and work preparation skills, group work and leadership skills, and understanding of the people and issues in their community—and do all of this using the language of images that they grew up with. In addition, by showing their tapes in public, the youth producers can make a meaningful contribution to the development of their community. The work seeks to maintain a balance between addressing the individual needs of young people and the collective needs of their community.

However, these possibilities can only be fully realized if the programs' guiding principles are based on a youth empowerment model; that is, teaching kids critical literacy requires that programs value and engage them as active participants in community problem-solving and as full partners in their own learning and growth. EVC professional developers have found from experience that working in programs that treat kids as passive recipients of knowledge or as potential delinquents to be controlled can be as difficult as any factory-model school.

Programs that don't see the importance of giving teens real responsibilities and real-world work often have a prevention model of work, whether it is violence prevention, dropout prevention, or drug abuse prevention, and tend to focus on the problems to be fixed rather than on the involvement of the youth and their community in fixing them. In these programs, one is more likely to witness the continuation in the after hours of the same kind of drill-and-practice literacy exercises that were given to the kids during their school day. Or the instructors design experiential projects, but it is the adults who are doing the work of deciding what questions to ask in their video news report or what message will be conveyed in their public service announcement, leaving little room for youth decision-making or ownership. Not a learner-centered approach, such a program emphasizes the role of adults as caretakers, problem-solvers, and deliverers of services, independent of a community context.

The paternalistic language of prevention is often used in government youth policy reports, as is evident in the report entitled *After-School Programs: Keeping Children Safe and Smart* that describes the purposes of its programs:

> First and foremost, after-school programs keep children of all ages safe and out of trouble. The after-school hours are the time when juvenile crime hits its peak, but through attentive adult supervision, quality after-school programs can protect our children . . . When the school bell rings, the anxiety for parents often just begins. They worry about whether their children are safe, whether they are susceptible to drugs and crime. (Chung, 2000, pp. 1–2)

It is important that the language of after-school programs, and the thinking behind that language, move beyond models of prevention and protection to develop young people as learners, citizens, and valuable resources for their community.

## YOUTH MEDIA AS CIVIC ENGAGEMENT

The 1989 United Nations Convention on the Rights of the Child (CRC), the most widely ratified convention in the world today, affirms that children and young people should have a say in matters that affect their lives and be involved in all processes that affect their well-being. The United States is the only country that has failed to ratify the convention (Irby et al., 2001).

In spite of the facts that the dominant political culture of this country opposes youth rights to autonomy and self-determination, and that the consumer media culture co-opts them, civic engagement is a growing trend among after-school community programs. There has been a growing awareness that engaging young people as active participants in their community is key to youth development and learning. Community service is becoming more common in schools, and new schools are being established by local community-based organizations with service as their theme. Organizations such as the Forum for Youth Investment, Jobs for the Future, and What Kids Can Do are among those documenting such community youth activities and promoting such an awarenesss.

At EVC, we have seen how providing youth with the technical, creative, and intellectual tools of media production and analysis gives great power and focus to their civic engagement. Through the process of conducting in-depth documentation, research, and public discussion of a community problem, EVC students have become engaged in and worked to change critical social issues in their lives, whether the subject of their documentary has been inequity in education (*Unequal Education: Failing Our Children*), homophobia (*Out Youth in School*), or African American/Jewish relations (*Blacks and Jews: Are They Sworn Enemies?*).

In *2371 Second Avenue: An East Harlem Story*, a student documented the housing conditions in which she and her family were living: a rat-infested building without heat or hot water. Through the process of asking questions and documenting these conditions, the student organized a rent strike and became the spokesperson for the rest of the tenants. After the student was interviewed and her tape was broadcast on television, the landlord sold the building, and conditions improved.

## SOCIAL CAPITAL

The power of these community youth media projects resides not solely in the community changes they have initiated but also in the civic skills, community connections, and relationships that the individual youth producers developed through the process. They built important relationships both with the adult mentors who facilitated their workshops and with the adults in the community whom they interviewed as part of their projects. Research has shown how important it is for youth to build relationships with adults, especially for kids who have learned from the streets to trust no one but themselves. As Milbrey McLaughlin (1993) describes, "The most essential contribution that youth organizations can make to the lives of young people is that of a caring adult who recognizes a young person as an individual and who serves as a mentor, coach, gentle but firm critic, and advocate"(p. 61).

The building of these connections in the community is part of the broader concept of social capital. Political scientist Robert Putnam describes social capital as:

> features of social organization, such as networks, norms, and trust, that facilitate coordination and cooperation for mutual benefit. . . . Successful collaboration in one endeavor builds connections and trust—social assets that facilitate future collaboration in other, unrelated tasks. (Putnam, 1993)

Social capital in and of itself is not sufficient to bring about social change; it must be combined with political capital. The notion of political capital is a measure of the influence a community has "to obtain resources, services, and opportunities from public and private sectors." When a community has high levels of social capital, its residents are more likely to assert their political capital (Zachary, 2001).

For students living in economically depressed communities, there are challenges on two levels. First, such students live in neighborhoods where much of the social fabric has been shredded by years of poverty, high crime, drugs, and disease. This is of particular concern in impoverished communities where high percentages of people have family members in prison, which leads to the further disruption of the social network of families and neighborhoods. In 1999, nearly 1.5 million children had at least one parent in state or federal prison (Cose, 2000).

Second, most schools and after-school programs don't teach students the habits and skills that would facilitate lasting connections to the viable people and institutions that do exist. Helping youth build relationships with community leaders is important for the students' future careers as well as for the continued vitality of grassroots community organizations.

Youth media projects address this problem in two ways. First, the documentary inquiry *process* gives the students multiple opportunities to practice developing relationships with community leaders. As a necessary part of their work, they learn the often-intimidating skills of writing, faxing, e-mailing, and calling adults to set up meetings and interviews with them. Finally, they experience how to sit across the table from an adult and have a conversation as partners sharing the common goal of improving their neighborhood. The adults they speak with, whether they run homeless shelters, programs for juvenile offenders, or AIDS prevention organizations, form part of a social network that becomes visible to the students only through their media project work.

Second, the media *product* that the students create has a value in itself in building social capital for the youth producers after the workshop or video program has concluded. More than a commercial or promotional video for a local business, students' tapes serve as catalysts for informing and organizing a community. Their work responds to the needs and serves the interests of the larger community. Instead of being seen only in terms of their deficits, as a problem for the adults in the neighborhood, the youth are seen in terms of their assets, as part of the solution. Through a combination of assistance from the adults in the youth program and the adults in the community organization featured in the documentaries, the students' work takes on the potential to open doors for higher education and employment; by itself, a résumé would not be able to open the same number of doors in quite the same way. Through their projects, the students are able to leverage people and institutions in their communities not only for the communities' own development, but also for their own individual progress. In this way, media production students find a unity of purpose in their learning as students, their work as artists, and their engagement as citizens.

## REIMAGINING THE SCHOOL DAY

Over the last decade there have been increasing efforts to link schools with after-school programs. On a federal level, the 21st Century Community Learning Center initiative has funded hundreds of such programs across the country. In New York City, the After School Corporation and the Fund for the City of New York's Beacon program have established scores of community-based programs that are housed in school buildings and serve kids in the nonschool hours.

On a practical level, they maximize the space and resources of schools and community organizations. On a more symbolic level, they represent the promise of combining the best practices of both worlds. This hope was expressed by Herb Sturz, the chairman of the After School Corporation in New York:

> The explosion in after-school programs . . . represents nothing less than a reimagining of the school day for the first time in generations . . . the key is to replace the "drill and kill" approach of the test-focused classroom with something that will "allow kids to learn and have fun at the same time." (*New York Times*, 2000)

In 1998, the Partnership for After School Education (PASE) was formed to promote this "reimagining of the school day," to build a field that offered an alternative to the "drill-and-kill" test-focused approach of the traditional classroom. PASE supports a range of ongoing professional development efforts to help create such alternatives.

As one after-school coordinator described what is possible,

> we strive to develop lessons that allow students to articulate their voices, histories, perspectives and beliefs. If children see themselves reflected in the curricula, and learn that their voices matter, then we believe they will be able to take action to improve the world in which they live and their own community. To help us do this, we go beyond academics to offer arts, recreation, and socially interactive games. This approach differs, at times, from the emphasis of the school. So the challenge is how to work together effectively (with the school partner)? (Fernandez, 2000, p. 2)

Young people stand to benefit if reform efforts from the school, after-school, and community development fields can join together. Such a working collaboration can provide a continuity of practice and principles across the day. Of course, the physical placement of an after-school program in a school building cannot in itself sweep away the institutional history and culture that has separated school from community and academic learning from social experience. It requires ongoing work on the part of the administration and teaching staff of both organizations to build a partnership rooted in common goals for the kids they serve.

The long-term vision for this collaboration is for there to be a cross-fertilization of each other's best practices. For example, one might hope that an after-school program culture can influence the school curriculum so that there is regular time to address students' family, emotional, and health problems, and that there is ample room in the curriculum for community and youth voices to be heard about those things that matter most in their lives—even if the students won't ever be tested on them. The hope is also that a school culture can influence an after-school program so that it engages kids in creative literacy and inquiry projects where learning and self-reflection are valued just as much as recreation and fun, and that while all youth projects are celebrated, young people also learn to critically assess their work and continually strive for high standards.

Media education can and should be a natural part of students' language, learning, and work experience in both of these settings. Perhaps kids can then have the opportunity—in the mornings, afternoons, and weekends—to develop the critical literacy skills needed to make and present media projects that explore those issues that shape their daily experiences, whether they are drawn from the world of the mass media, school, or their surrounding community.

## DOCUMENTATION, REFLECTION, AND STAFF DEVELOPMENT

To build and sustain such an environment during and after school, staff need to be engaged in an on-going process of professional development. In addition to offering training workshops on a whole range of teaching and youth development strategies, this requires that regular meeting time be set aside just for talking about, and exploring in depth, issues of teaching, learning, and youth development. Ideally, youth, teachers, and program staff should be in the habit of documenting their own work and routinely reflecting on the challenges, victories, and lessons learned through it. This helps codify the practices of the school and the after-school program, and preserve continuity in the program in spite of staff turnover.

As we have seen, in the hands of students video is a powerful tool for documentation and reflection. It is certainly also a powerful tool in the hands of teachers, staff, and community leaders. Taping students in class and in their after-school activities and discussing the tapes in a supportive group environment helps to build a culture of collaborative, participatory research and reflection.

This kind of working collaboration can go a long way toward bridging the disconnect, alienation, and language gap discussed earlier. There are many good examples of such school/community partnerships, and it is certainly possible for them to continue to spread, provided that there is enough funding for resources and staff development, and enough attention paid to ensuring the democratic participation of all the partners—especially the youth.

## STUDENT VOICES

### Reflections

Trying to assess the long-term impact of EVC's video work on the youth who participate is a complicated business. Just tracking down where the students live is a challenge. Addresses and phone numbers change, and some don't have working phones. And once they are found, it is still not easy to determine the impact. Each kid takes away something different. For some, the social and emotional dimension of the experience was most powerful. They said they developed a stronger sense of accomplishment, purpose, and possibility. Others were moved in a more intellectual way, growing new ways of asking questions, looking at the media, and expressing their ideas. In the midst of the project, they can't always articulate just how it is changing them. It's just another experience that gets filed away, another part of their older, more mature selves. Sometimes it is not until months or even years later when, upon reflection, a memory surfaces of a lesson learned that stayed with them, and then it takes on a sharpness and importance that it didn't have at the time.

Joseph, one of the students who worked on the *Young Gunz* documentary, visited my office recently. Home for the weekend from college at the State University of New York at New Paltz, he was exploring summer job possibilities. He was handsome as ever, but more self-confident, articulate, and sure of himself. He was majoring in Communications and Black Studies. He proudly told me that he was recently elected president of his student association.

I asked him what, from this vantage point some five years later, he felt he learned.

"It taught me the importance of working with a team. Trying to achieve one common goal. That experience itself is just invaluable to me. Also, working with a diverse group of people every day, people from different backgrounds, genders, races. We worked three or four hours every day . . . When we started, we didn't know each other. Everyone was quiet. I thought to myself a lot, 'How I am going to get through this?' I sometimes wondered what I was doing there. We really came together by the end. I remember working together over the Christmas break. We would all hang out. Outside of EVC. At the end of the process we were almost like a family. . . . It shows that the possibilities are endless. It taught me a lot about sacrifice. We came in a lot during our winter break to finish it. Once everyone could see it actually materializing, everyone wanted to make it the best as possible . . . It helped me transition to college. You have to work in college on group projects and presentations. The chances of working with someone of a different race or a different gender are high. Because of my experience at EVC, I had a leg up. I had some previous experience. It definitely helped me. . . . It gave me self-confidence. Just having that understanding, 'Yes, I can do this. I am capable.' It went a long way to helping me. No one can ever take that away from me."

### East City High School

It's a year after the Doc Workshop. I saw familiar faces, but also many new ones. There continues to be very high turnover of teaching staff. Seven teachers left last year and another seven or eight say they won't return to the school in the fall. And both the principal and the assistant principal are leaving as well.

But another teacher team-taught a video class during the spring semester. She was pleased to report that the students produced public service announcements on such issues as safe sex and littering. Julius told me he was accepted to Virginia College. He will be the first in his family to ever go to college.

Majandra plans to go to St. John's to study journalism. Her best friend Monica is still in school, even after she gave birth to a baby boy last fall.

Gail spoke of last year's class and how she was moved by the experience of going out to interview a psychologist as part of her class's documentary on teen suicide. "I remember this one day real well. We went to Ninety-first Street and First Ave. The doctor talked about suicidal teens. I remember it so much because I had friends who almost committed suicide. It helped me get a clearer understanding of the actions that they [the doctors] take toward it. The actions that they take and that they show you to also follow."

### Speaking Out at the Screening

Another group of EVC students had a screening recently. Even after 17 years of screenings, I still find each one such an inspiring and moving experience, with these kids in a line across the stage, squinting into the lights, up in front of their friends, family members, teachers, and complete strangers who fill the public library media center auditorium. They always start out the evening full of hesitation, awkwardly standing there, trying to field the questions that come at them. And by the end of the discussion, they somehow stand taller, full of self-confidence and conviction.

The documentary was about how the mainstream media misrepresents teenagers as violent superpredators when in fact the real rate of youth crime has been steadily decreasing and is at its lowest point since 1966. When asked about why they chose to make their tape about that particular topic, one student said: ". . . because we knew the media has a great impact on everyone. We knew the juvenile justice system is going through some bad times. And we especially wanted to connect those two. How the media could influence people's perspectives: therefore making the public more scared of youth, therefore cracking down on juvenile crime."

Another student quickly added, "We wanted to use the media against the media."

Someone from the audience asked: "With all the overtime and everything [you had to put into your project], if you had the opportunity to do it again, would you?"

A girl standing all the way on the left of the line of students took the microphone. English is her third language, but she spoke it with great passion: "Well, probably for me, I would do it. Because I chose this internship because I wanted to do something different with my life, you know. Doing this has been a really great thing for me, especially as a youth. I'm a teen. I want to prove to the whole world about my opinion, and what the media is saying about me that is really wrong. Because you know, they judge me by who I am, and the way I look. So I will do it again, if I have to stay overtime. I don't mind. It doesn't matter to me, I will do it. Because if they say youth are useless and they are bad. We can think better than them. And we can be smarter than them by doing this kind of work. By showing this kind of work, it is like we are fighting back for our rights. If I had a chance, I will do it again."

As she finished, the audience burst into applause.

After the screening ended, I walked into the warm Manhattan night and thought, yes, there has been progress. Some lives have been really transformed; some futures have opened up. We have come quite far. But damn, we still have a long way to go.

# References


Annie E. Casey Foundation. (July 1999). "Improving school–community connections: Ideas for moving toward a system of community schools." *Foreword*. Baltimore, MD: Annie E. Casey Foundation.

Aufderheide, Patricia. (1993). *Media literacy: A report of the National Leadership Conference on Media Literacy*. Washington, D.C.: The Aspen Institute.

Bailey, Ian, and Mary Vallis. (December 1, 2000). "Computers disrupt classrooms: Study, fixing high-tech tools keeps teachers from their primary tasks." *National Post*. Retrieved from http://pacific.commerce.ubc.ca/kbe/december1.pdf

Barry, Dave. (July 28, 1996). "'Dave's' cigarettes have him fuming." *SouthCoast Today.com*. Retrieved from http://www.s-t.com/daily/07-96/07-28-96 e02li154.htm

Beck, Allen, and Thomas P. Bonczar. (1997). *Lifetime likelihood of going to state or federal prison*. Washington, D.C.: Bureau of Justice Statistics.

Bikerts, Sven. (1994). *The Gutenberg elegies*. New York: Fawcett Columbine.

Borja, Rhea. (December 5, 2001). "Black State Lawmakers Target 'Gap'." *Education Week* [on-line]. Retrieved from http://www.edweek.org/ew/newstory.cfm?slug=14caucus.h21

Bruner, Jerome. (1986). *Actual minds, possible worlds*. Cambridge and London: Harvard University Press.

Brunner, Cornelia, and Bill Tally. (1999). *The new media literacy handbook: An educator's guide to bringing new media into the classroom*. New York: Anchor Books, Doubleday.

Buckingham, David. (1997). "News media, political socialization and popular citizenship: Towards a new agenda." *Critical Studies in Mass Communication, 14,* 344–366.

Cahill, Michelle. (1997). *Youth development and community development: Promises and challenges of convergence*. Community and Youth Development Series, Volume 2. Takoma Park, MD: The Forum for Youth Investment, International Youth Foundation.

Chung, An-Me (June 2000). *After-school programs: Keeping children safe and smart*. Washington, DC: U.S. Department of Education.

Considine, David. (December 1990). "Media literacy: Can we get there from here?" *Educational Technology*, 27–32.

Cose, Ellis. (November 13, 2000). "America's prison generation." *Newsweek*, 40–49.

Crary, Jonathan (1999). *Suspensions of perception: Attention, spectacle, and modern culture.* Cambridge, MA: The MIT Press.

Cuban, Larry. (1986). *Teachers and machines: The classroom use of technology since 1920.* New York and London: Teachers College Press.

Dale, David. (August 20, 2001). "Angels to angst: The ages of adolescents." *Media Monitor* [on-line] Retrieved from http://old.smh.com.au/news/0108/20/entertainment/entertain8.html

Dewey, John. (1916). *Democracy and education.* New York: MacMillan.

Dewey, John. (1934). *Art as experience.* New York: Minton, Balch, and Co.

Dewey, John. (1976). *The School and Society in The Middle Works, 1899–1924,* Volume 1, 1899–1901. Edited by Jo Anne Boydston. Carbondale: Southern Illinois University Press.

Eco, Umberto. (1986). *Art and beauty in the middle ages.* New Haven and London: Yale University Press.

Ewen, Stuart. (1988). *All consuming images: The politics of style in contemporary culture.* New York: Basic Books.

Fernandez, Kathy. (Fall 2000). "Approaching yes: Afterschool programs, schools, and community partnerships." *PASE* newsletter, issue 17, pp. 2, 10.

Fisherkeller, JoEllen. (2002). *Growing up with television: Everyday learning among young adolescents.* Philadelphia: Temple University Press.

Gabler, Neal. (1998). *Life the movie: How entertainment conquered reality.* New York: Alfred A. Knopf.

Gee, James P. (1996). *Social linguistics and literacies: ideology in discourses.* London: The Falmer Press.

German Commission for UNESCO. (January 22, 1982). *Grunwald declaration on media education.* Grunwald, Federal Republic of Germany: UNESCO's International Symposium on Media Education.

Greene, Jay P. (January 16, 2002). "Graduation statistics: Caveat emptor." *Education Week* [on-line] Retrieved from www.edweek.org/ew/newstory.cfm?slug=18greene.h21

Greene, Maxine. (1988). *The dialectic of freedom.* New York and London: Teachers College Press.

Haeberle, Austin. (Fall 2001). "A report from NAMAC's online salon." *NAMAC MAIN newsletter,* pp. 1, 5.

Halpern, Robert, Sharon Deich, and Carol Cohen. (May 2000). *Financing afterschool programs.* Washington: D.C.: The Finance Project.

Heath, Shirley Brice. (1983). *Ways with words.* Cambridge: Cambridge University Press.

Heins, Marjorie, and Christina Cho. (2002). *Media literacy: An alternative to censorship.* New York: Free Expression Policy Project.

Henry J. Kaiser Family Foundation. (November 1999). *Kids & media @ the new millennium, executive summary.* California: Author.

Hirsh, E. D. Jr. (Summer 2001). "Overcoming the language gap." *American Educator, 25*(2), 4–7.

Irby, Merita, T. Ferber, and K. Pittman, with J. Tolman and N. Yohalem. (2001). *Youth action: Youth contributing to communities, communities supporting youth. Com-*

*munity and Youth Development Series, 6*. Takoma Park, Maryland: The Forum for Youth Investment, International Youth Foundation.

Justice Policy Institute press release. (August 29, 2001). "Students report school crime at same level as 1970's but use of suspension doubles."

Kangisser, Dianne. (December 1999). *The third arena: Afterschool youth literacy programs*. New York: Robert Bowne Foundation.

Levine, Joshua. (April 21, 1997). "Badass sells." *Forbes, 159*(8), 142.

McDill, Edward L., Gary Natriello, and Aaron M. Pallas. (1986). "A population at risk: Potential consequences of tougher school standards for student dropouts." In Gary Natriello (Ed.), *School dropouts: Patterns and policies* (pp. 106–147). New York and London: Teachers College Press.

McLaughlin, Milbrey W. (1993). "Embedded identities: Enabling balance in urban contexts." In Shirley Brice Heath and Milbrey W. McLaughlin (Eds.), *Identity and inner-city youth: Beyond ethnicity and gender* (pp. 36–68). New York and London: Teachers College Press.

McNeal, James. (1999). *The kids market: Myths and realities*. Ithaca, NY: Paramount Market Publishing.

*The merchants of cool*. (February 27, 2001). Produced by Barak Goodman and Rachel Dretzin for *Frontline*. Boston: PBS.

Oppenheimer, Todd. (July 1997). "The computer delusion." *The Atlantic Monthly, 280*(1), 45–62.

Packaged Facts. (Nov. 1, 2000). *The U.S. urban youth market: Targeting the trendsetters*. New York: Packaged Facts, a division of MarketResearch.com. Retrieved from http://www.marketresearch.com/product/display.asp?SID=35113880-232841740-267856276&ProductID=186560&kw

Poe-Yamagata, Eileen, and Michael A. Jones. (April 2000). "Building blocks for youth: And justice for some." *National Council on Crime and Delinquency*, 24.

Postman, Neil. (1994). *The disappearance of childhood*. New York: Vintage Books.

Putnam, Robert D. (March 21, 1993). "The prosperous community: Social capital and public life." *The American Prospect*. Retrieved from http://www.prospect.org/print/V4/13/putnam-r.html

Reese, Shelley. (January/February 1998). "KIDMONEY: Children as big business." *Arts Education Policy Review, 99*(3), 37–41.

St. John, Mark. (1999). *"Wait, wait! don't tell me!": The anatomy and politics of inquiry*. New York: The City College Workshop Center.

Shlain, Leonard. (1998). *The alphabet versus the goddess: The conflict between word and image*. New York: Viking.

Silverfine, Debby. (1994). *Set in motion, the New York State Council on the Arts celebrates 30 years of independents*. New York: New York State Council on the Arts.

Snyder, Howard N., and Sickmund, M. (1999). *Juvenile offenders and victims: 1999 national report*. Washington, D.C.: Office of Juvenile Justice and Delinquency Prevention.

Spring, Joel H. (1972). *Education and the rise of the corporate state*. Boston: Beacon Press.

*Teenage Research Unlimited press release*. (2000). "Teens spend $155 billion in 2000." Retrieved from http://www.teenresearch.com/PRview.cfm?edit_id=75

Tyack, David. (1974). *The one best system*. Cambridge: Harvard University Press.

Tyack, David, and Larry Cuban. (1995). *Tinkering toward utopia: A century of public school reform*. Cambridge: Harvard University Press.

Tyner, Kathleen. (1998). *Literacy in a digital world: Teaching and learning in the age of information*. Mahwah and London: Lawrence Erlbaum Associates.

We Interrupt This Message, Youth Force. (Winter 2000). *In between the lines: How the New York Times frames youth*. New York: Youthforce, We Interrupt This Message.

Weber, Lillian, and Beth Alberty. (1997). *Looking back and thinking foreward: Reexaminations of teaching and schooling*. New York: Teachers College Press.

Wigginton, Elliot. (1986). *Sometimes a shining moment: The Foxfire experience*. New York: Anchor Press/Doubleday.

Wilgoren, Jodi. (January 24, 2000). "The bell rings but the students stay, and stay." *New York Times*, p. A1.

Zachary, Eric, and shola olataye. (2001). *A case study: Community organizing for school improvement in the South Bronx*. New York: Institute for Education and Social Policy.

Zollo, Peter. (June 1999). "Why teens are a hot market." *American Consumers Newsletter, New Strategist Publications*.

# *Suggested Works*


Baudrillard, Jean. (1988). "Consumer society" in *Selected writings* (pp. 31–44). Mark Poster, editor. Stanford, California: Stanford University Press.

Boyle, Deirdre. (1997). *Subject to change: Guerrilla television revisited*. Oxford and New York: Oxford University Press.

Fine, Gary Alan, and Jay Mechling. (1993). "Child saving and children's cultures at century's end." In Shirley Brice Heath and Milbrey W. McLaughlin (Eds.), *Identity and inner-city youth: Beyond ethnicity and gender* (pp. 120–146). New York and London: Teachers College Press.

Foster, Michelle. (1997). "Ebonics and all that jazz: Cutting through the politics of linguistics, education, and race." *The Quarterly of the National Writing Project*. *19*(1), 7–12.

Heath, Shirley Brice, and Milbrey W. McLaughlin. (1993). *Identity and inner-city youth: Beyond ethnicity and gender*. New York: Teachers College Press.

Heintz, Katharine E. (Fall 1994). "Smarter than we think—kids, passivity and the media." *Media Studies Journal, Children and the Media, 8*(4).

Hugo, Victor. (1964). *The hunchback of notre dame*. New York and Scarborough, Ontario: Signet Classics.

Kress, Gunther. (1997). *Before writing rethinking the paths to literacy*. New York and London: Routledge.

Martin, Henri-Jean. (1994). *The history and power of writing*. Chicago and London: University of Chicago Press.

Nance-Nash, Sheryl. (October 1998). "How to keep your brand modern." *Business 2.0*, Retrieved from: http://www.business2.com/articles/mag/0,1640,6422, 00.html

Ong, Walter J. (1982). *Orality and literacy—the technologizing of the word*. New York and London: Routledge.

Parenti, Michael. (1992). *Make believe media: The politics of entertainment*. New York: St. Martin's Press.

Passmore, John. (1972). "On teaching to be critical." In R. F. Dearden, P. H. Hirst and R. S. Peters (eds.), *Education and reason: Part 3 of education and the development of reason*. London and Boston: Routledge and Kegan Paul.

Shamberg, Michael, and Raindance Corporation. (1971). *Guerilla television*. New York: Holt, Rinehart, and Winston.

Stein, Charles. (October 1998). "Can they stay cool?" *Business 2.0*. Retrieved from: http://www. business2.com/articles/mag/0,1640,6437,FF.html

*Teen Fact Book 1997–98*. New York: Channel One Network.

U.S. Census Bureau, Public Information Office. (Revised 2000). "Profile America" [Transcript]. Retrieved from http://www.census.gov/pubinfo/www/radio/who329.htm

U.S. Department of Education. (2000). *21st century community learning centers: Providing quality after school learning opportunities for America's families* [on-line]. Retrieved from http://www.ed.gov/21stcclc/

Wartella, Ellen. (Fall 1994). "Electronic childhood." [Special Issue]. *Media Studies Journal, Children and the Media, 8*(4).

Williams, Raymond. (1974). *Television: Technology and cultural form.* Hanover and London: University Press of New England.

Woodward, Emory H. (2000). *Media in the home 2000: The fifth annual survey of parents and children.* The Annenberg Public Policy Center of the University of Pennsylvania.

*Young Gunz.* (1997). Directed by Joan Jubela. Produced by the Educational Video Center.

# Index

# *About the Author*

**Steven Goodman** is the founder and executive director of the Educational Video Center. He has worked as a media educator and producer since 1980. Trained as a journalist at the Columbia Graduate School of Journalism, Goodman has produced social documentaries and written on youth media and education for numerous publications including *Education Week, Contemporary Art and Multicultural Education, The Independent Film and Video Monthly*, and *Youth Today*. He has taught in New York City alternative high schools and designed and conducted graduate media education courses at New York University, the University of London Institute of Education, the University of Southern Maine, Ohio University/Ohio SchoolNet, and the City University of New York. On weekends, he can often be found coaching his children's little league baseball and soccer teams where he lives in Huntington, Long Island.